# HUSKY

# Allied Invasion of Sicily 1943

*Shawn Nutter*

WORLD WAR II HISTORY 1
BENNINGTON, VERMONT
2013

## ON THE COVER

*M4 Medium Tanks enter Palermo, Sicily.*

First Edition published in 2013 by the Merriam Press

First Edition

Copyright © 2013 by Shawn Nutter
Additional material copyright of named contributors
Book design by Ray Merriam

ISBN 978-1491064740
Merriam Press #WH1-P

This work was designed, produced, and published in the United States of America by the

Merriam Press
133 Elm Street Suite 3R
Bennington VT 05201-2250
USA

E-mail: ray@merriam-press.com
Web site: merriam-press.com

The Merriam Press publishes new manuscripts on historical subjects,
especially military history and with an emphasis on World War II,
as well as reprinting previously published works,
including reports, documents, manuals, articles and other materials on historical topics.

This volume also available as an Adobe Acrobat PDF file, #WH1-PDF, for $9.99 postpaid.
To order, see the Merriam Press web site or write to the address above.

# Husky

## Allied Invasion of Sicily
## 1943

### The Allied Strategic Debate

HUSKY[1] was an operation born in controversy. During the so-called Second Washington Conference in the early summer of 1942, an acrimonious debate raged between the British and their new American allies over the future strategic course of the war against the European Axis powers. General George C. Marshall, Chief of Staff of the United States Army, espoused the view that the Allies could successfully confront the European Axis only by means of an amphibious invasion of Western Europe, and that consequently no operations which might detract from this goal should be undertaken.[2] In a sharply worded memorandum to President Franklin Roosevelt, Prime Minister Winston Churchill attacked Marshall's position:

> No responsible British military authority has so far been able to make a plan for September, 1942 which had any chance of success unless the Germans become utterly demoralized, of which there is no likelihood. Have the American Staffs a plan? If so, what is it? What forces would be employed? At what points would they strike? What landing-craft and shipping are available? Who is the officer prepared to command the enterprise? What British forces and assistance are required? If a plan can be found which offers a reasonable prospect of success, His Majesty's Government will cordially welcome it and will share to the full with their American comrades the risks and sacrifices. This remains our settled and agreed policy... But in case no plan can be made in which any responsible authority has good confidence, and consequently no engagement on a substantial scale in France is possible in September, 1942, what else are we going to do? Can we afford to stand idle in the Atlantic theatre during the whole of 1942?[3]

Of course, the Allies did not "stand idle" during 1942. In November of that year, American forces came ashore in French North Africa to join with the British to begin the process of driving the Axis from the African continent. Nevertheless, the controversy over the primacy and urgency of an invasion of Western Europe to Allied strategy continued, finding its next venue at the Casablanca Conference, conducted in that North African city between January 14 and January 23, 1943. The Casablanca Conference produced a decision favoring Operation HUSKY. In preparation for the Conference, the U.S. Joint Chiefs of Staff promulgated a memorandum setting forth their basic strategic concept for 1943 in December, 1942.[4] Their view was that the "primary effort" of the Allies should be directed against Germany by rapidly building up in the United Kingdom sufficient forces for a land offensive against Germany in 1943. With regard to North Africa, the U.S. Chiefs believed that once the Axis had been expelled, the Allies should establish large air bases in North Africa for the purpose of beginning "intensive" air operations in order to drive the Italians out of the war. However, only forces sufficient to secure the Allied position would remain in the theatre; the remainder would be sent to the United Kingdom to take part in the invasion of Western Europe.

The British position on the matter of North Africa was quite different. It was conditioned by British concern over the perceived perils of invading a European continent still indisputably under German mastery. One member of the British Chiefs of Staff, John Slessor, took the view that there was no hope of establishing a substantial force on the mainland, to say nothing of confronting and defeating the *Wehrmacht*,

---

[1]   The code name adopted for the Allied invasion of Axis-occupied Sicily in July, 1943.

[2]   U.S. Department of State, *Foreign Relations of the United States* [hereinafter "*F.R.U.S.*"], *Conferences at Washington, 1941-1942 and Casablanca, 1943*, G.P.O. 1968, Memorandum Marshall to Roosevelt, June 23, 1942, pp. 473-475.

[3]   *Ibid.*, Memorandum Churchill to Roosevelt, June 20, 1942, pp. 461-462.

[4]   *Ibid.*, Memorandum by the United States Chiefs of Staff, December 26, 1942, pp. 735-738.

"until German resistance had been softened up from the air." The previous September, Air Chief Marshal Sir Charles Portal, the British Chief of Air Staff, had produced a memorandum in which he set forth his position on the future course to be followed by the Allies for the remainder of the war. There were three alternatives available, namely (a) to invade Western Europe precipitously, with as much force as could be mustered in a short period of time, sufficient to overcome the *Wehrmacht*; (b) to crush German resistance through the air, only after which would invasion be undertaken; or (c) a mixture of (a) and (b), in which both air and land forces would be amassed, without a specific invasion plan. Both Portal and Slessor favored the second approach, although they saw themselves and their allies pursuing the third. The second view became the official position of the British Joint Planners in October, 1942

The first of the military meetings associated with the Casablanca Conference convened on January 14, 1943 with Marshall urging a general agreement on the distribution of Allied effort between the Atlantic and Pacific theatres. Four days later the meetings continued, with "an apparently wide divergence of opinion on basic strategy." According to Slessor, "[T]he morning's discussion did not go at all well and at times became uncomfortably warm." The sensitive topic of the Allies' German policy generated all of the energy. After the lunch break, however, the parties were able to agree upon a memorandum, drafted by Slessor, which cleverly balanced the efforts of the Allies in the major theatres.

The British Chiefs prepared two lengthy memoranda in which they set out their own arguments for how the war should be prosecuted in 1943.[5] They suggested that two alternatives were available, namely (a) to concentrate on building up a force in the United Kingdom "of sufficient size to invade the Continent," or (b) to "devote our main effort towards undermining the foundations of German military power" while simultaneously building up forces in the United Kingdom for a "return to the Continent as soon as German powers of resistance have been sufficiently weakened." The first of these alternatives corresponded to the American plan, and the British Chiefs had no hesitancy in criticizing it in no uncertain terms:

...the adoption of this strategy would mean a relaxation of pressure on the Axis for 8 or 9 months with incalculable consequences to the

Russian Front and at the end of the period no certainty that the assault on France could, in fact, be carried out. Or even if it were carried out, that it would draw out land forces from the Russian Front.

The British plan, then, contemplated the application of continuous pressure on the Axis by all available means. With reference to North Africa and the Mediterranean region, the British plan meant that every effort would be made to drive Italy out of the war, so as to stretch the *Wehrmacht* to its limits. In contrast to the American concept, which called for Allied consolidation in North Africa and its use as a base for air strikes against Italy and Germany, the British scheme required the seizure of Sicily or Sardinia in order to increase the pressure on Italy.

President Roosevelt and the American Joint Chiefs of Staff had prepared for the Conference at a White House meeting on January 7, 1943.[6] In response to Roosevelt's suggestion that "we should meet the British united in advocating a cross-Channel operation," General Marshall made the revealing statement that "there was not a unified front on that subject, particularly among our Planners." Marshall went on to say that while the American Chiefs favored an invasion of Western Europe over any Mediterranean operation, "the question was still an open one." The Chiefs specifically discussed the alternative Mediterranean targets of Sicily and Sardinia. Interestingly, while Marshall rejected both choices in favor of an assault on the Brest Peninsula, both Admiral Ernest J. King, Chief of Naval Operations, and General Henry H. Arnold, Chief of U.S. Army Air Forces, indicated a preference for an attack on Sicily.

The ambivalence of Marshall and the other American Chiefs was openly displayed nine days later at a meeting of the Combined Chiefs of Staff. Marshall began the discussion aggressively, saying that the Combined Chiefs should "reorient" themselves "and decide what the 'main plot' is to be. Every diversion or side issue from the main plot acts as a 'suction pump.'"[7] Marshall urged that while an operation against Sicily looked advantageous because of the "excess number of troops in North Africa," the role of such an undertaking in the overall strategic plan should be determined before a final decision was made. Notwithstanding this expression of disdain for the Sicilian invasion by Marshall, and persistent questioning by the other American Chiefs regarding the

5    *Ibid.*, Memorandum by the British Chiefs of Staff, January 2, 1943, pp. 738-741; Memorandum by the British Chiefs of Staff, January 3, 1943, pp. 741-752.

6    *Ibid.*, Joint Chiefs of Staff Minutes of a Meeting at the White House, January 7, 1943, pp. 505-514.
7    *Ibid.*, Meeting of the Combined Chiefs of Staff, January 16, 1943, pp. 580-594.

availability of sufficient landing craft, by the end of the meeting the Combined Staff Planners had been directed to "reexamine the British plan for HUSKY... *and to calculate the earliest date by which the Operation could be mounted*" (emphasis added). Two days later, the Secretaries of the Combined Chiefs of Staff circulated a memorandum setting forth the Combined Chiefs' recommendations for the conduct of the war in 1943.[8] In this document, the occupation of Sicily is specifically called for, while provision is made for assembly in the United Kingdom of forces sufficient to re-enter Europe "as soon as German resistance is weakened to the required extent."

On January 22, 1943 the Combined Chiefs established the high echelon of command for the Sicilian campaign, identifying General Dwight D. Eisenhower as the Supreme Commander, with British General Sir Harold Alexander as his Deputy Commander-in-Chief. Two additional British officers, Admiral Andrew B. Cunningham and Air Chief Marshal Arthur W. Tedder, were named Naval and Air Commander respectively. The Combined Chiefs further instructed Eisenhower to set up a special operational and administrative staff, with its own Chief of Staff, for the planning and preparation of the invasion.[9]

## THE STRUGGLE FOR AN ALLIED PLAN

General Eisenhower attended the Casablanca Conference only briefly. On January 15, after a harrowing journey in which his B-17 lost two engines, and he ended the trip in a parachute harness, he reported on the progress of the campaign in Tunisia. The decisions of the Combined Chiefs of Staff first came to his knowledge when he received his copy of the official minutes of the conference. Eisenhower had anticipated that the Allies would pursue some further action in the Mediterranean at the end of the Tunisian campaign, so that even before the Casablanca Conference his staff had been tentatively planning an operation against Sardinia and Corsica. The main effect of this exercise was to convince Eisenhower that possession of Sicily would be of much more significance to the Allies than the seizure of Sardinia and Corsica, since control of Sicily would greatly facilitate control of the Mediterranean shipping lanes.

Broadly speaking, the decision of the Combined Chiefs of Staff in favor of an operation against Sicily was taken in order to secure Allied lines of communication in the Mediterranean, move the Italians in the direction of abandoning the Axis, and assist the Russians by drawing away as many German forces as possible. It was also hoped that the invasion would persuade Turkey to enter the war on the side of the Allies. The Combined Chiefs went so far as to tentatively set the date for the invasion during the favorable period of the July moon, ultimately the period July 10 through July 14.

The view of the British Chiefs and their planners was that the campaign would last six weeks, and that their effort would be mounted from North Africa rather than from the United Kingdom. British planners believed that U.S. forces would require the use of the ports in Algeria and Tunisia, and that accordingly the British and Commonwealth forces would be limited to the ports of Haifa, Alexandria, Port Said, Tripoli and Malta. In their view, use of these ports would reduce the number of assault craft necessary for the British force from 190 to 65. The downside of this arrangement was that the invasion would be delayed by a month's time, owing to the crowding which would result. The July timetable was affirmed, however, when the U.S. Chiefs guaranteed that some of the Tunisian ports would be made available to the British forces.

The Combined Chiefs' directive assigned Eisenhower responsibility for the detailed planning, preparation and execution of the operation, and gave him limited authority for the target date. The Combined Chiefs retained authority for whether an earlier invasion date, during the favorable period of the June moon, might be met, while directing Eisenhower to advise them of any difficulties which might preclude a July invasion. The Chiefs gave Eisenhower a deadline of March 1, at which time he was to confirm that there would not be a delay in the launch date beyond the period of the August moon.

In spite of having set a tentative date for the invasion of early July, the Combined Chiefs almost immediately instructed Eisenhower to work toward a target date during the favorable period of the June moon. This was based on an assumption that the Tunisian campaign would be completed by April 30. After an intensive study of the question, Eisenhower and his staff reported to the Chiefs on February 11 that such a date was out of the question, since it would mean reducing the amount of training time to an unacceptable level. Eisenhower's conclusion was based on three considerations, namely (1) that the U.S. 3d Infantry Division, identified already as a part of the invasion force, was to be used in Tunisia as well, and could not be ready in June, even if the Tunisian campaign were wrapped up by the end of April; (2) that the preparation of airfields in Tunisia

8   *Ibid.*, Memorandum by the Secretaries of the Combined Chiefs of Staff, January 18, 1943, pp. 760-761.

9   *Ibid.*, Meeting of the Combined Chiefs of Staff, January 22, 1943, pp. 680-686.

would require at least four weeks, and that it was still uncertain whether the Tunisian ports would be available to mount the invasion; and (3) that insufficient landing craft were available to adequately train the armored units for the invasion.

The Combined Chiefs rejected Eisenhower's report on February 19, stating that "all preparations must be pushed with the utmost vigor to achieve" the June date. Churchill was particularly adamant that "[I]t is absolutely necessary to do this operation in June. We shall become a laughing stock if, during the spring and early summer, no British and American soldiers are firing at any German and Italian soldiers." On March 20 Eisenhower reported the unanimous opinion of all his commanders that the tentative date of June 10 would be impossible to meet, and that in fact no date before July 10 would be possible, unless there were a total and immediate Axis collapse in Tunisia. Again on April 10 he confirmed that a date of June 10 was not feasible, but advised that "the state of our preparations should make the July date possible." The Combined Chiefs approved Eisenhower's decision for a July D-day on April 13.

Some of the American forces that would be used in the Sicilian campaign had previously been detailed for action in the event of intervention by the Germans from Spain. The so-called Northern Task Force, under General Mark Clark, had developed plans for action either in Spanish Morocco or the Iberian Peninsula, and substantial forces were maintained in Algeria and French Morocco for this eventuality. But the decision in favor of the HUSKY operation quickly unraveled the Northern Task Force. Eisenhower stripped it of forces in the United Kingdom that had been designated for possible use in a Spanish campaign, reassigned its staff for HUSKY and appropriated its shipping and landing craft for the upcoming invasion.

As Alexander remained absorbed with the Tunisian campaign, Eisenhower appointed Major General C.H. Gairdner to head a special combined planning staff. Major General A.A. Richardson succeeded Gairdner in May. The combined staff was organized according to the British system, since it had been determined that the ground campaign would be commanded by a British general, namely the deputy Commander-in-Chief of the operation. Eisenhower's headquarters was in the St. George Hotel in Algiers, but because of a lack of space at that venue, the combined planning staff occupied the Ecole Normale in the Algiers suburb of Bouzarea. The headquarters for FORCE 343 (later the U.S. Seventh Army) first located in Rabat, French Morocco, and later moved to Mostaganem, Algeria. While the naval headquarters was also located in Algiers, with Admiral Cunningham and U.S. Admiral Hewitt installed at the St. George Hotel (165 miles from Mostaganem and 555 miles from Rabat), the subordinate naval commanders were located 200 miles away at Oran and Bizerte, respectively 200 miles and 335 miles from Algiers. The combined planning staff was designated H.Q. FORCE 141, derived from the room number at the St. George Hotel where the Allied Force Headquarters (A.F.H.Q.) had first met to discuss the Sicily operation. It later became the headquarters for the 15th Army Group. It had no indigenous intelligence section, but was forced to rely on A.F.H.Q. for intelligence which had to be obtained by a special liaison section, described by Eisenhower as "an arrangement which resulted in a not altogether satisfactory production of intelligence in the earlier period." The planning situation was a major detriment to Eisenhower. Eisenhower experienced frustration from the very beginning. In a letter to Marshall dated January 30, 1943, he reported that Alexander had just announced his decision to accept the command arrangement for HUSKY.

> ...although I know he is not particularly happy about it. I immediately replied, asking him to name his Chief of Staff and to come here in person as quickly as he can. These two campaigns have definitely merged into one, and it is high time that Alexander got on the job and took the tactical reins in his hands.[10]

The bane of Eisenhower's existence quickly became what he identified as the "committee system of command" favored by his three British subordinates.[11] He decried this tendency among Alexander, Cunningham and Tedder, and complained that "it seems impossible for the British to grasp the utter simplicity of the system that we employ." Eisenhower made clear that he considered the committee system to be a "definite invasion" of his authority, and advised Marshall that he would not permit it to control and direct "any important military venture."

Many commands subordinate to FORCE 141 were widely scattered, some as much as a thousand miles from one another. Practical problems resulted. Naval requests for photographic reconnaissance of the beaches on Sicily were not given timely consideration. The air force failed to give the navy prints of the sorties that were actually flown, when such prints

10    Joseph P. Hobbs, *Dear General: Eisenhower's Wartime Letters to Marshall*, Johns Hopkins Press, 1971, p. 97.
11    *Ibid.*, Eisenhower Letter to Marshall, February 8, 1943, pp. 99-101.

were widely distributed to military commands without any responsibility for the landing shores. The result was that naval planners were seriously hampered in their study of beach characteristics. When the FORCE 141 plans were ultimately complete, the army and navy planners of the Western Naval Task Force were withdrawn from the FORCE 141 planning staff. Henceforth there was poor communication between the air planners and their army and navy colleagues, and indeed the development of the air plan was unknown to the navy or the military. When finally the air plan was made known, it was lacking in information about either fighter cover or fighter support during the landing phase, though it did provide data on air force equipment and supplies scheduled to be brought ashore. There was also serious disagreement among the air force, army and navy over the issue of pre-invasion targets. Seventh Army Headquarters, in conjunction with the navy, assembled a list of bombing targets suitable for attack prior to D-day. When its creators provided the list to the air planners, the latter found the targets unsuitable and rejected the list. This step seriously disconcerted the military and naval planners, since they regarded the targets they had selected as threats to the success of the amphibious assault. Following a great deal of controversy, a list of targets "satisfactory to the air force" ultimately issued. A similar circumstance prevailed with respect to the bombing agenda for D-day, which was not disclosed to the naval and army commanders until the time the invasion fleet sailed for Sicily. Because of this circumstance, the naval and military commanders went to the combat zone with almost no knowledge of what their air force colleagues would contribute in either the landing phase or afterwards. The air force failed to communicate to them even the most general information about the air situation, so that the army and navy commanders had no information about the extent to which the air force had succeeded in disrupting enemy communications or reducing his beach defenses.

One of the problems confronting Eisenhower and the FORCE 141 staff was that the island of Sicily was obviously much more accessible to Axis forces than it was to those of the Allies. The Tactical Appreciation prepared by Eisenhower's staff showed that there were six train ferries operating daily across the Straits of Messina between Sicily and the Italian mainland. There were four termini on Sicily at Messina, and three on the mainland so that the ferry service could deliver 40,000 men, or in the alternative 7,500 men and 750 vehicles, in a 24 hour period. In fact, at the time the Tactical Appreciation was done, there were never more than two such ferries in oper-

ation, but the staff also reckoned that there was a steamer service with a 24 hour capacity of 12,000, as well as an air transport service capable of lifting 1000 tons of supplies per day. Sicily possessed 19 airfields suitable for use by the Axis.

The combined planning staff also recognized that Messina was the most important objective on the island. However, direct assaults upon it, either between Messina and Palermo to the West, or between Messina and Catania to the south, were out of the question. The Straits were closed to Allied shipping and beyond the range of fighter cover, as were the areas to the west and south of Messina. For obvious reasons, landing areas on Sicily were limited to beaches where direct fighter cover could be provided, between Avola and Gela in the southeast and between Sciacca and Marinella in the west. In those areas there were no major ports to provide unloading facilities. For this reason the terrain was thought to favor the Axis. The available beaches were not particularly suitable to motor transport, as they were of soft sand in a gentle gradient. They were also narrow, and gave way, with the exception of the plain surrounding Catania, to terrain that was alternately hilly and mountainous, and which would obviously confine tanks and motor transport to the few available roads. Eisenhower and his staff rightly concluded that some of the terrain would be so difficult as to require the use of pack animals.

In order to get a sufficient force onto the island to effectively confront the enemy, it would be necessary for the Allies to capture suitable ports. Since Messina would be unavailable, Eisenhower planned to seize the ports of Syracuse and Catania in the east, and Palermo in the west. In this regard, Catania and Palermo were recognized as essential, for without them it would not be possible to maintain the forces necessary to capture the island. Since all of these ports were beyond the range of fighter cover, the first objective of the assault forces would be the capture of the airfields in both the southeast and west of the island, in order to allow the air cover to be extended in such a way as to support capture of the ports.

The combined planning staff quickly resolved that two task forces would be necessary, one from the west and one from the southeast. However, while it would be easier to provide air cover to the western approach, this avenue was at the same time more exposed to attack by enemy aircraft based at Sardinia. Such vulnerability was not present for the southeastern approach, which had the added advantage of lending itself to surprise, since the progress of a naval force along this course would more nearly approximate a normal convoy. The Tactical Appreciation also suggested that the western landings would be more difficult. Such a situation normally would have suggested a simultaneous attack, designed to disperse the enemy's resources to the maximum degree. There were strong arguments, however, to support the staggering of the attacks, with the southeastern assault to be staged first. The element of surprise was one important consideration favoring staggered attacks, as was the notion that a move first in the southeast would tend to draw off enemy resources from the west. The deciding consideration in favor of simultaneous attacks, however, was the decision to employ airborne troops in advance of the landings. The airborne units were to be used to soften the enemy's beach defenses, since the other commitments of both the naval and air elements were so great that those elements could not be relied upon to reduce the beach defenses. Indeed, the Tactical Appreciation placed the role of the paratroops in softening the defenses higher on the priority list than even the seizure of the island's airfields.

The planned use of airborne troops, however, exacerbated Eisenhower's timing problems, since whereas the use of parachutists implied moonlight, the naval forces required darkness for their approach. Indeed, it was essential that the landings occur in the two hours of darkness before dawn, so that adequate anti-aircraft defenses could be established ashore before first light. The only suitable compromise was that the invasion be launched in the so-called "favorable period" of the moon, in effect its second quarter, when there would be moonlight in the early period of the night, and complete darkness after midnight. Accordingly, when the month of July was determined to be the most likely target date for the operation, the deadline of the 10th of the month was automatically determined.

A working plan for placing the Allied forces on Sicily first appeared in February, 1943. On February 12, the basic plan developed by British planners and accepted by the Combined Chiefs, was distributed to the operational planning staff, where it was recognized as preliminary and tentative. This initial plan envisioned two simultaneous assaults, one in the southeast and one in the west. There were to be follow-up landings at Catania and Palermo, with ten divisions safely on the island within a week of the initial assault. Indeed, the plan concentrated on the seizure of the ports of Palermo and Catania, rather than on the destruction of enemy forces. This original draft had at least two major faults, namely (1) it called for dissipation of the assault force by requiring immediate seizure of the widely dispersed airfields on the island, and (2) it did not call for the two principal

task forces to be mutually supporting. The latter fault was potentially disastrous, as it would allow the defenders to concentrate on one landing force at a time in an effort to throw it back into the sea.

General Alexander appreciated the plan's shortcomings, and considered concentrating both assault forces in one attack against the southeast corner of Sicily, although he concluded that such an approach was not feasible because it would not yield enough port facilities to support the operation. General Bernard L. Montgomery, the putative commander of British ground troops in HUSKY, found other reasons to object to the initial plan. In its original conception, the plan called for British Eighth Army to land not only on the eastern shore, but also around on the southwestern side near the ports of Licata and Gela. The far more significant ports of Augusta and Syracuse lay on the eastern side, yet the plan called for only about one third of the Eighth Army's strength to be committed to this portion of the assault. For this reason, Montgomery declared in March, 1943 that he could not accept the plan in its present embodiment.

In spite of Eisenhower's resolve, matters did not appreciably improve. On March 3, he lamented to Marshall that

> HUSKY planning is most involved and difficult. Since, by direction, we are using for the operation the British system of command, the whole arrangement – in high echelons – presents intricacies and difficulties that cause me a lot of headaches.[12]

He reiterated this theme less than a month later, calling the HUSKY planning "onerous and difficult." He reported having made changes in the plan against his better judgment, simply in order "to satisfy Alexander and Montgomery." Apart from his problems in interacting with his subordinates, Eisenhower expressed his fears about the outcome of the operation, claiming that the Allies were "skating close to the edge of unjustified or at least dangerous risk" owing to the unavailability of sufficient combat loaders.[13]

Early in the planning stage the Western Task Force (later U.S. Seventh Army) and the Eastern Task Force (later British Eighth Army) were identified as FORCE 343 and FORCE 545 respectively. On March 18 representatives of both FORCE 343 and FORCE 545 attended a conference at HQ

---

[12] *Ibid.*, Eisenhower Letter to Marshall, March 3, 1943, pp. 107-108.

[13] *Ibid.*, Eisenhower Letter to Marshall, March 29, 1943, pp. 107-108.

FORCE 141, resulting in an outline plan issued March 25. The plan envisioned staggered assaults, beginning with British troops landing on beaches extending from Syracuse to Gela. Thereafter, one U.S. division would land between Sciacca and Mazzara on D plus 2. The remaining U.S. divisions would land on D plus 5 immediately west of Palermo. There were to be five British divisions and four American divisions. Eisenhower disliked this plan, since in his view it dispersed Allied forces to an unacceptable degree. Moreover, Alexander and Montgomery had previously convinced him that Allied forces were spread too thin, and that FORCE 545 could not capture the airfields in the Catania/Gela sector without being reinforced with an additional division. Eisenhower debated for the next six weeks deciding which was the greater risk—the failure to take the Catania/Gela airfields, or the failure to capture Palermo early and put it to use as a port.

Eisenhower concluded that HUSKY would fail without the early capture of the Catania/Gela airfields. The "guiding principle" in planning therefore became the taking of sufficient "insurance" for the rapid capture of these targets. The first proposed solution to this conundrum was a compromise. In view of the shortage of shipping, the preferred alternative seemed to be to transfer one American division from the Western to the Eastern Task Force. This could only be done by canceling the southwestern assault scheduled for D plus 2. This would permit the shifting of the U.S. 3d Infantry Division to the Gela landing sector. This solution was inherently flawed, however, because the southwestern assault force, now substantially weakened, had the objective of taking the Sciacca/Mazzara area and its airfields, to enable close air support for the Palermo landings scheduled for D plus 5. Those landings were not feasible until the Catania/Gela fields in the southeast had been taken. The D plus 5 target for the Palermo assault therefore had to be abandoned in favor of a date "determined by the progress of FORCE 545."

Neither were the British keen for the plan in question. They feared that if the capture of Palermo were delayed, the Germans would turn their continued possession of it to good account, and that the *Luftwaffe* would belabor the Eastern Task Force from those southwestern air bases which would now be left untouched. In light of these concerns, on March 25, 1943 the British suggested to the Combined Chiefs of Staff that an additional division "must be provided by hook or by crook" in keeping with the original plan for the early capture of Palermo. The Combined Chiefs informed Eisenhower of the British view of the case on the next day. Eisenhower at least tentatively restored the original plan, including an assault on D plus 2 by an American division in the southwest sector. He also increased the reserve force at Malta from a Brigade Group to a full infantry division. This unit was neither assault trained nor assault loaded as a result of the shortage of adequate shipping.

Montgomery suggested an alternative approach in which the landing in the Gela-Licata area would be eliminated. In this way, he would gain at least another division for the assault on the eastern side of the island, and his forces would be united, and thus have greater striking power. Montgomery's amended plan would mean that certain enemy airfields would not be seized. This subjected it to an immediate and vociferous attack from Allied air and naval commanders. Air Chief Marshal Tedder argued that the failure to land in the Gela-Licata area and secure the airfields in that sector would greatly weaken the Allied position, so much so that the risk of losing large assault vessels would be greatly increased. Admiral Cunningham shared Tedder's views.

General Alexander sided with Montgomery, agreeing to strengthen Eighth Army's assault on the east coast by moving all of its troops to that side of the island. He endeavored to soften the blow to his air and naval commanders by taking the U.S. 3d Infantry Division from its American task force, placing it under Montgomery's command, and assigning it to land in the Gela-Licata sector. To avoid any resultant attenuation in American strength, Alexander proposed that Seventh Army's landings be delayed several days so as to strike at the Axis forces while they were fully engaged with the British.

Although General Patton objected to the loss of 3d Infantry Division on the ground, among others, that his own forces would be unacceptably weakened, General Eisenhower nevertheless approved Alexander's new plan because he considered success in the southeast quadrant of Sicily to be vital to the operation.

The British eventually mitigated the controversy, at least in part, by supplying an additional division, along with its transport, to Montgomery, and releasing the 3d Infantry Division to General Patton. However, Alexander remained wedded to the concept of follow-on landings. Now, 3d Infantry Division would land on D plus 2, while the remainder of the American force would come ashore in the Palermo sector on D plus 5.

Both Eisenhower and the British took the view that in the event "substantial" German forces were encountered in the assault zone, "our operation offered scant promise of success." In this context, "substantial" was defined to mean anything more than two divisions. Moreover, while the Allies "naturally" denigrated the combat efficiency of the Italian formations on the island, they also believed that the presence of "substantial" German forces would enhance the resolve of the Italians. The Tactical Appreciation suggested that two German divisions were indeed on the island, and the possibility existed that they might be reinforced from either the Italian mainland or Tunisia. Eisenhower was so concerned with this contingency that he felt it his "duty to warn the Combined Chiefs of Staff that in that event our venture would become risky indeed." He did so twice, on March 20 and April 7, and was rebuked for his apparent lack of confidence in Allied arms. Churchill vociferously denounced Eisenhower's views on this issue.

> Months of preparation, sea power and air power in abundance and yet two German divisions are sufficient to knock it all on the head. I do not think we can rest content with such doctrines...it is perfectly clear that the operations must either be entrusted to someone who believes in them, or abandoned. I trust the Chiefs of Staff will not accept these pusillanimous and defeatist doctrines from whoever they come...I regard the matter as serious in the last degree. We have told the Russians that they cannot have their supplies by the northern convoy for the sake of HUSKY, and now HUSKY is to be abandoned if there are two German divisions (strength unspecified) in the neighborhood. What Stalin would think of this when he has 185 German divisions on his front, I cannot imagine.

As might be expected, the Allied force commanders remained skeptical of Alexander's plan, in spite of its changes, or perhaps because of them. Because Montgomery was preoccupied with operations in Tunisia, on April 17 he sent his chief of staff, Major General Francis ("Freddie") de Guingand, to meet with the British planning staff in Cairo. There, de Guingand reviewed the most recent plan variant with Lieutenant General Miles C. Dempsey, commander of British XIII Corps. He concluded that the plan did not provide for sufficient concentration of force to assure Allied success. Montgomery then flew to Cairo on April 23 to confer with de Guingand and others. The next day he informed Alexander of his misgivings, which were based on his apprehension that the plan wrongly assumed that the Germans and Ital-

ians would not mount a serious defense of Sicily. "Never," said Montgomery, "was there a greater error."

Montgomery wanted to concentrate his forces in a landing in the Gulf of Noto, to the south of Syracuse. He pointed out that this operation would receive adequate air cover from aircraft based on Malta. With such a landing, Eighth Army would be capable of capturing, in short order, the ports of Syracuse, Augusta and Catania. Tedder and Cunningham, however, were not satisfied, and wanted to extend the British beachhead to Gela, in order to cover the airfields at Comiso and Ponte Olivo. Montgomery insisted that he would need yet further assault forces to accomplish this expanded task.

In view of the continued lack of consensus, Alexander convened a conference in Algiers on April 29. Lieutenant General Oliver Leese acted as Montgomery's chief of staff, since de Guingand had been injured in an air crash. In addition to presenting Montgomery's views, Leese suggested that the Allies scrap the bifurcated attack of the original plan in favor of a combined U.S.-British assault in the southeast corner of the island. In this scheme, U.S. forces would land on either side of the Pachino peninsula, while the British came ashore in the Gulf of Noto. Both Cunningham and Tedder rejected Leese's suggestion, because it would leave untouched a substantial number of airbases, creating a heavy burden for Allied air units and placing Allied shipping at risk. They insisted that the southeastern assaults move immediately to seize the airfields at Comiso, Ponte Olivo and Biscari. Montgomery balked at this notion, arguing that his forces were not sufficient to secure the use of these fields; the best that he could hope to do would be to deny them to the enemy.

For Eisenhower, this evidently irreconcilable conflict was yet further evidence of "the fundamental weakness of our entire strategic plan." Planning for the operation had thus reached an impasse. Eisenhower sought to break it by assembling the commanders in Algiers for another conference on May 2. Montgomery appeared in person to argue for the new plan first expressed by General Leese. On May 3 Eisenhower stopped the "tinkering" of his staff, junking the original plan in favor of Montgomery's. He threw out the idea of a southwestern assault on D plus 2, as well as the notion of assaults west of Palermo on D plus 5. Instead the Western Task Force was to be shifted to the southeastern landing. In so doing, Eisenhower accepted the risks associated with failure to bring Palermo online as a functioning port, thereby casting aside the evident teaching of the North African operation that an invading force must have at its disposal a functioning port within 48 hours of landing. Eisenhower relied on three elements in assuming this risk, namely (1) the more favorable summer weather; (2) the certainty of sea and air superiority; and (3) the availability of the *DUKW*, a technical innovation which had been lacking in the *TORCH* landings. The Combined Chiefs of Staff approved the new plan on May 13. It called for the entire American force to be concentrated from Licata eastward to the Pachino peninsula; the British force would land between the peninsula and Syracuse. In effect, the Allies had abandoned two of the main tenets of the original plan of the Combined Chiefs, which called for quick seizure of the major ports and the airfields. The new plan therefore left unresolved the concerns which Admiral Cunningham and Air Chief Marshal Tedder had all along expressed. Indeed, apparently no one but its author liked the Montgomery plan, and Eisenhower was persuaded to accept it because his logistics officers told him that the *DUKW*s , now available in quantity, would enable them to adequately supply the Seventh Army.

## THE INVASION OF SICILY AND ALLIED GRAND STRATEGY

On May 12, 1943, the same day on which the Allied field commanders approved the final plan of invasion for Sicily, the Combined Chiefs of Staff met at the White House with Roosevelt and Churchill. The latter began the discussion by asserting that once HUSKY had been successfully concluded, the prime objective in the Mediterranean must be to drive Italy out of the war by the best available means. He recounted a litany of beneficial developments—closer ties between the Allies and Turkey, enhanced activity on the part of Balkan guerrillas, which would in turn require either a German retreat from the region or the withdrawal of considerable German forces from Russia, and the elimination of the Italian fleet—all of which would perforce transpire once Italy were driven from the war.[14]

The Prime Minister spoke of additional post-HUSKY objectives. The first of these Churchill termed "taking the weight off Russia." He pointedly reminded his audience that there were 185 German divisions on the Eastern Front. The "prodigious" effort that this required of Russia, at a time when the western Allies were not fully engaged with the German Army, was making the Allies beholden to Stalin. Churchill abhorred this condition and wanted to make an end to it. In his view, the best means of do-

ing so was to force Italy out of the war, thereby requiring the Germans to devote a substantial numbers of troops "to hold down the Balkans."[15]

The third objective, upon which both Churchill and Roosevelt agreed, "was to apply to the greatest possible extent our vast Armies, Air Forces, and munitions to the enemy. All plans should be judged by this test." Churchill postulated that the *HUSKY* operation would be completed by the end of August. What, he asked rhetorically,

> should these [Allied] troops do between that time and the date 7 or 8 months later, when the cross-Channel operation might first be mounted? They could not possibly stand idle, and he could not contemplate so long a period of apparent inaction. It would have a serious effect on relations with Russia, who was bearing such a disproportionate weight.[16]

Roosevelt asked the same question, but reached a different conclusion. He admitted having an aversion to the idea of invading Italy, on the theory that this could lead to an attrition of Allied forces that would favor Germany. It was nevertheless true that approximately 25 Allied divisions were now committed in the Mediterranean, a fact which raised the obvious question of how such troops could be used in 1943, as opposed to being left idle. The easy solution would be to commit these forces to an occupation of Italy, a notion that Roosevelt thought ill-considered. Instead, a survey should be conducted to determine the relative cost of such an occupation as opposed to the cost of achieving the same result by mounting an air offensive from either Sicily or the heel and toe of Italy. In any case, he pointed out, the Allies would have a surplus of manpower, and these men should be immediately committed to the build-up for the cross-Channel invasion of Europe. Roosevelt urged that the Allies now commit themselves to an operation in northwestern Europe in the spring of 1944. This approach, he said, was the best method of taking weight off Russia.[17]

On May 13, 1943, the Combined Chiefs of Staff convened at the Federal Reserve Building in Washington, D.C. in connection with the Third Washington Conference. Each of the Staffs brought with them their senior planning officers, who were to attend the general discussions on global strategy, including forthcoming operations in both Europe and the Pacific, and prepare a detailed agenda thereafter.

---

[14]  *F.R.U.S., Conferences at Washington and Quebec 1943*, G.P.O. 1970, pp. 25-26.

[15]  *Ibid.*, p. 27.
[16]  *Ibid.*
[17]  *Ibid.*, pp. 30-32.

The first topic of discussion was the invasion of Sicily.

General Marshall and General Sir Alan Brooke, Chief of the Imperial General Staff, first considered the likely length of the Sicilian campaign. Brooke opined that if the operation were launched on 10 July, it should be completed within thirty days. Marshall advised that his planners had estimated that the revised plan just approved might take until the middle of September.[18] Portal immediately upstaged this quibbling over dates by offering his opinion that "...the *weakness* of the new plan lay in its failure to seal the island to reinforcements."[19] While Portal's analysis was astute, those present might reasonably have concluded that his comments might have been better left unsaid, particularly in view of the fact that the planning for Sicily was being coordinated by his colleague Alexander.

A more general discussion of overall strategy ensued. After a series of digressions into areas of lesser significance, the participants gradually returned to the issue which most clearly revealed the area of principal disagreement between the Allies, namely whether their strategy should concentrate ultimately on Italy and the "soft underbelly" of Europe, or the concept of a cross-channel attack. On the American side, King and Admiral William D. Leahy, Roosevelt's personal Chief of Staff, expressed their view that while "it was generally agreed that the elimination of Italy would have extremely valuable results," it might be unwise to divert to or maintain in the Mediterranean forces which could be used in a cross-channel assault or as a prelude to such an attack. If we weakened our potentialities for a cross-Channel assault by continuing to confine forces to the Mediterranean, it might preclude a major effort against Germany on the Western Front.[20]

Brooke replied that "if we did not continue operations in the Mediterranean, then no possibility of an attack into France would arise."[21] Seeing that the discussion was now "getting to the heart of the problem," Marshall interjected a passionate argument against remaining bound to a Mediterranean-centered strategy. He noted that initial estimates of requirements were always exceeded. The North African campaign, for example, "had sucked in more and more troops," the numbers of which had been ultimately limited only by the availability of shipping. The tendency of a campaign to create a vacuum into which one's forces flowed exacerbated the negative

aspects of the maxim that once an operation was undertaken, it must be backed to the hilt. In this vein, Marshall expressed his deep concern that the landing of ground forces in Italy would create a vacuum which would prevent the Allies from assembling sufficient forces in the United Kingdom for a successful cross-Channel attack. If the Allies persisted in undertaking further operations in the Mediterranean then for the rest of 1943 and most of 1944 they would be committed to a Mediterranean policy. According to Marshall, this would prolong the Pacific war, and thus delay the ultimate defeat of Japan, "which the people of the U.S. would not tolerate."[22]

Brooke expressed a diametrically opposed opinion, arguing that to cease operations in the Mediterranean after the Sicilian campaign was concluded would lengthen the war. The essence of his argument was that since Russia was the only one of the Allies with substantial ground forces, the proper strategy for Britain and the United States must be to assist her as much as possible. At present, the western Allies could best do this by "continuing in the Mediterranean."[23]

In answer to a suggestion by Marshall that eleven U.S. divisions could be made available in the United Kingdom by April, 1944, Brooke launched into an even more negative assessment. He asserted that

> ...these combined forces would only be sufficient to hold a bridgehead and would not be large enough to debauch into the Continent. Now was the time when action was required to relieve the pressure on Russia. No major operations would be possible until 1945 or 1946, since it must be remembered that in previous wars there had always been some 80 French Divisions available on our side. Any advance towards the Ruhr would necessitate clearing up behind the advancing Army and would leave us with long lines of communications. Our air force in U.K. was at present largely on a static basis though it was being converted now for use with the expeditionary force. The British manpower position was weak, and to provide the necessary rearward services for continental warfare, two of our twelve divisions now in U.K. would probably have to be cannibalized.[24]

Brook's remarks prompted Marshall to inquire quite bluntly whether the British Chiefs of Staff re-

18    *Ibid.*, p. 36.
19    *Ibid.*, p. 37; emphasis added.
20    *Ibid.*, p. 43.
21    *Ibid.*

22    *Ibid.*, p. 44.
23    *Ibid.*
24    *Ibid.*, p. 45.

garded operations in the Mediterranean to be the key to an Allied victory in the European theatre of war. Portal replied that he and his colleagues believed that unless the greater portion of the German Army were tied down in Russia or the Balkans, an invasion force of twenty to twenty-five divisions would not be able to achieve important results on the Continent. He went on to argue that the capacity of the Allies to operate on the Continent in the future depended upon their present ability to aid the Russians. But unless the Allies could knock Italy out of the war in 1943, it would not be possible for them to reenter northwest Europe the following year. Marshall flatly disagreed, stating that if the Allies ever were to get sufficient forces in the United Kingdom for the invasion, they must begin at once. "Further operations in the Mediterranean would... create a vacuum which would constitute a drain on our available resources." [25]

The British Chiefs were not persuaded by Marshall, and continued to press home their attack. Brooke expressed his fear that a Russian collapse "would prolong the war for many years." He urged that the Russians would benefit far more if the Allies were to attack Italy immediately. Such a course was preferable to preparing for cross-Channel operations that could not be a significant consideration until the following year. In Brooke's opinion, the "problem" was how best to compel the Germans to withdraw substantial forces from the Eastern front. As between the alternative solutions under discussion, a prompt attack in the Mediterranean would promise immediate favorable results, as compared with a proposed invasion of northwestern Europe in 1944, "which might not even then be possible." [26] Marshall responded by suggesting that continuous Allied air operations in the Mediterranean would cripple the Italians and tie down large numbers of German troops, since the enemy command could not safely ignore the peninsula as a potential Allied invasion route. He returned once again to the theme that land operations in the Mediterranean would needlessly prolong the European war, thereby further delaying a decision in the Pacific. In the face of this, however, the British remained adamant. Portal said that the Italians could not be knocked out of the war through air action alone, and that in any case, "[O]ur object was to assist Russia, and we must achieve this object as early as possible." [27]

The obstinate attitude of the British Chiefs of Staff on the question of Mediterranean land operations reflected the position of the Prime Minister. In a telegram to President Fra[nklin D. Roosevelt of] April 5, 1943, Churchill provid[ed...] a copy of a memorandum that [he had di-]rected to the British Chief of Staffs [... as a] channel for thought and planning." I[n it he] assumed that the Sicilian invasion wou[ld begin no] later than July 10, and that the Allies woul[d outnum-]ber the Axis forces by a factor of two to one. Based on these "givens," he concluded that the battle for the island would last a week, "after which one might reasonably expect that the bulk of the enemy's forces would be destroyed, captured or driven into the mountains." [28]

For the Prime Minister, the most important issue raised by this scenario involved the future deployment of Allied forces in the aftermath of this success. Churchill was ready with an answer, and expressed it vigorously in the memorandum. He began by placing the Sicilian operation in the context of his vision for the prosecution of the war:

> Hitherto the capture of HUSKY-land has been regarded as an end in itself; but no one could rest content with such a modest and even petty objective for our armies in the campaign of 1943. HUSKY-land is only a stepping stone, and we must now begin to study how to exploit this local success. [29]

Although Churchill then urged consideration of every possible alternative for the employment of Allied troops, it is clear from his memorandum that such alternatives did *not* include preparation for a cross-Channel attack in the following year. Indeed, the only alternatives that he discussed were an operation in the Eastern Mediterranean, including an attack on the Dodecanese in an effort to bring Turkey into the war on the side of the Allies, or an assault on Italy, Sardinia and Corsica. Which of these paths the Allies should follow would be dictated by the extent to which the Germans remained engaged in Italy. In Churchill's opinion, however, even if the Italians remained in the war and were able to rely on German assistance, the Allies should attempt to gain lodgments on both the heel and toe of Italy as soon as they had concluded their operation in Sicily. Churchill concluded the memorandum, and his message to Roosevelt, by stating that "the mere capture of HUSKY-land will be an altogether inadequate result for the Campaign of 1943." [30]

The disagreement at the highest level was shared

---

25   *Ibid.*
26   *Ibid.*, p. 46.
27   *Ibid.*

28   *Ibid.*, pp. 12-13.
29   *Ibid.*, p. 13.
30   *Ibid.*, pp. 13-14.

...uld command the forces with whose ...a idleness after the conclusion of HUSKY ...sevelt and Churchill were so concerned. On May 14, 1943, General Walter Bedell Smith, Eisenhower's Chief of Staff, presented the Combined Chiefs of Staff with a memorandum comprised of two papers both of which were directed to the question of what operations should be undertaken following HUSKY. The Operations Division of Allied Force Headquarters in Algiers had drafted the first, which represented the views of both General Eisenhower and Admiral Cunningham. Air Chief Marshall Tedder had prepared the second, intending it to be a dissenting opinion. Eisenhower expressed the view that after the conclusion of HUSKY there would be two courses of action available to the Allies, either an invasion of Italy or the seizure of Sardinia and Corsica as bases for Allied air operations. He and Cunningham favored the latter, because it would not commit the Allies to the mainland and the possibility of "a major campaign the duration and requirements of which it is not possible to foresee." Tedder said that he could not agree with either the paper or its conclusions because it exaggerated the value of Sardinia to the Allies and underestimated the difficulties which would attend its capture, while it ignored the value that Italy would have for the Allies as an airbase for heavy bomber attacks on most of the vital industrial production centers in Germany.[31]

The British Chiefs of Staff presented their own memorandum to Roosevelt and Churchill on May 14, in which they set forth their recommendations for Allied operations between the completion of HUSKY and the invasion of France. A fundamental premise of the memorandum was Churchill's argument that once Sicily had been conquered, Allied forces in southern Europe could not stand idle for nine or ten months until preparations for the invasion of France had been completed. The British Chiefs, in a surprisingly forceful statement of their strategic view, declared that the Allies must force Italy to capitulate by means of a "relentless" attack. Indeed, they stated flatly that an Italian surrender, "more than any other single event, would hasten the early defeat of Germany." The fall of Italy would require the Germans to withdraw significant forces from Russia to defend the Balkans, Greece and France, thus setting in motion a chain of events whose ultimate effect would be the collapse of the Third Reich. They therefore recommended that preparations be made for an invasion of the toe of Italy immediately after the conclusion of HUSKY,

and that in addition General Eisenhower have available alternative plans for an operation against the heel of Italy, and for the capture of Sardinia. The Chiefs also spelled out a plan for occupying essential portions of Italy in the event of its collapse after HUSKY. They closed their memorandum with the statement that "[I]f we take these opportunities, we shall have every chance of breaking the Axis and of bringing the war with Germany to a successful conclusion in 1944.[32]

The conceptual battle over war fighting strategy was well articulated in a pair of memoranda prepared by the respective British and American Joint Planning Staffs. The British submitted their paper, entitled "British Plan for the Defeat of Axis Powers in Europe," to the Combined Chiefs of Staff on May 17, 1943.[33] It was a highly detailed analysis of the strategic and tactical elements that would be necessary to defeat the Axis in Europe as soon as possible. It began with a lengthy section on the proposed invasion of northwestern Europe. The cast of mind of the British planners was capsulized in paragraph 21 of the first section:

21. After a successful HUSKY the greatest aid we could give to Russia, and thereby inflict greatest injury which could be done in Germany, would be to tear Italy from the Axis.[34]

With this premise in mind, the British planners spent the remaining two substantive sections of the memorandum detailing the sequence of anticipated Allied operations in the Mediterranean after the completion of *HUSKY* and the bearing that these operations would have on Anglo-American preparations in the United Kingdom for the forthcoming cross-Channel attack. In their conclusion, they summarized the British plan for defeating Germany, beginning with the following commentary:

55. To concentrate our efforts after the completion of HUSKY solely upon ROUNDUP (codename for an early invasion of the continent with minimal forces) is to forego the initiative to the enemy for some months, to adopt a defensive attitude on land and to allow Germany to concentrate for the defense of France and the Low Countries against our invasion.

56. Our plan for the defeat of Germany is

[31]   *Ibid.*, pp. 256-257.

[32]   *Ibid.*, pp. 257-261.
[33]   *Ibid.*, pp. 261-272.
[34]   *Ibid.*, p. 265.

therefore:

a. *To eliminate Italy...*[35]

The means enunciated to achieve this goal was a combination of air action and either an invasion of the Italian mainland or landings in both Sardinia and Corsica. The British planners gave April, 1944 as the target date for an invasion of northwestern Europe under this scenario.

The contrasting view of the American Joint Staff Planners could be seen in the very title of their memorandum, "Defeat of Germany from the United Kingdom," which they provided to the Combined Chiefs of Staff on May 18, 1943.[36] The language in which they couched the "problem" addressed by their memorandum also betrayed the fundamentally different viewpoint which the Americans brought to the issue of Allied strategy after the conclusion of the HUSKY operation:

1. To present a plan for the defeat of Germany (showing the course of operations and their feasibility) by concentrating the biggest possible invasion force in the United Kingdom as soon as possible.[37]

Likewise, among the significant assumptions made by the American planners were the notions that the Allies would conduct no amphibious operations in the Mediterranean after the close of the Sicily operation, and that Allied air operations in that theatre would be limited to the protection of shipping and the bombing of Italy.

The Americans made themselves quite explicit as to the position of Italy in their plans in their analysis of general strategic considerations for the European and Mediterranean theatres in the years 1943 and 1944. In order to achieve their objective, the American planners considered four points to be essential, namely: (a) the bomber offensive from the United Kingdom; (b) the maximum build-up of forces in England, for the purpose of invading northwestern Europe in the spring of 1944; (c) keeping Russia in the war; and (d) maintaining air operations in the Mediterranean at a minimum after HUSKY, so as not to prejudice the bomber offensive, the pre-invasion build-up and the invasion itself. These elements were at the heart of the American concept for the defeat of Germany, which was in turn based upon several premises, prominent among which were the following:

a. Defeat of the Western Axis by means of an invasion from the Mediterranean is unsound strategically and logistically.

\* \* \*

e. We further believe: that the elimination of Italy is not a prerequisite for the creation of conditions favorable for ROUNDUP; that the elimination of Italy may possibly be brought about without need of further amphibious operations in the Mediterranean, by a successful HUSKY and an intensified bomber offensive against Italy—in fact Italian defection might precede HUSKY; that if, after HUSKY, Italy has not surrendered or collapsed, the advantages to be gained in eliminating Italy by conducting further amphibious operations are not worth the cost in forces, shipping, amphibious equipment, and time; ...

f. Experience in TORCH and in preparation for HUSKY has shown that once an operation, even though admittedly secondary, is directed, the desire to insure its success leads to increasing demands for greater and greater forces...[38]

In view of the foregoing, it is not surprising that among the conclusions reached by the American planners was that Mediterranean operations subsequent to HUSKY should be limited to the air offensive, because any other operations would drain off forces necessary for the pre-invasion build-up, "thus needlessly prolonging the war."[39]

[35]   *Ibid.*, p. 272; emphasis added.
[36]   *Ibid.*, pp. 272-281.
[37]   *Ibid.*, p. 273.

[38]   *Ibid.*, pp. 274-274.
[39]   *Ibid.*, p. 281. Four days earlier (May 14, 1943), the United States Chiefs of Staff circulated among the Combined Chiefs a memorandum prepared by the United States Joint Staff Planners entitled "Conduct of the War in 1943-1944." As to the Mediterranean, the memorandum recommended that after the completion of HUSKY, the Allies conduct only limited operations in that theatre, primarily by means of air attacks on Italy from Mediterranean bases. The U.S. planners stated categorically that the level of forces committed in the Mediterranean must "not...prejudice the success of a cross-Channel operation in 1944." The U.S. Chiefs of Staff circulated with the memorandum a brief note in which they said that "[T]he enclosed study was prepared by the United States Joint Staff Planners and meets with the approval of the United States Chiefs of Staff." *F.R.U.S., I The Third Washington Conference,* "Study by the United States Joint Staff Planners. Conduct of the War in 1943-1944." May 14, 1943, pp. 227-229.

The Combined Chiefs discussed the HUSKY operation and the problem of Italy in general at their meeting of May 18, 1943 in Washington.[40] Although technically the Chiefs had received both memoranda prepared by the respective Joint Planning Staffs, only the British memorandum was on the agenda. As a result, the Chiefs ultimately deferred action on the issues at hand until both memoranda could be studied further by the American Chiefs. In spite of this, the rift between the Western Allies over the Mediterranean question made itself apparent. General Marshall pointed out inconsistencies in the British position, noting that the British memorandum began with the assumption that an April, 1944 cross-Channel operation would be impossible, but concluded with the thesis that an April, 1944 target date could be agreed upon, provided that Mediterranean operations were undertaken in the interval. Brooke replied that it was the British view that an April, 1944 deadline could not be met *unless* Mediterranean operations were undertaken. The British Chiefs believed that such operations would influence the strength of German opposition to be encountered, and would in fact be essential in creating a situation in which an invasion of northwestern Europe could take place. According to Brooke, the German build-up of forces in western Europe would greatly exceed that of the Allies if Mediterranean operations were not undertaken to divert German reinforcements. In the British calculation, forcing Italy out of the war would be the key element in wasting German reserves and allowing the concentration of Allied forces for the Continent to exceed that of the enemy.[41]

Marshall was unrelenting. He said that he was "extremely doubtful" whether the contemplated Mediterranean offensive, if successful, would permit sufficient forces to be made available in the United Kingdom to exploit that success. He expressed his concern that Mediterranean operations might of necessity be of a greater magnitude than expected, with the result that the forces necessary for the cross-Channel invasion would be reduced. In that event, the Allies might only be capable of an operation that contemplated no opposition from the enemy. In reply, Brooke suggested that at most the Mediterranean operations would reduce the Allied concentration in the United Kingdom for cross-Channel operations by three and a half to four divisions. In his view, this was a "cheap price" to pay for the diversion of German strength that would be caused by knocking Italy out of the war. He said that eliminating Italy from the war was the best way of rendering aid to Russia in 1943. Finally, he challenged Marshall's thesis that an Italian operation would lead to a continuous and as yet incalculable drain on Allied resources by arguing that the operations visualized for the Mediterranean theatre were not interdependent and that the "cost value" of each such operation could be individually assessed at the appropriate time. Before voting to table the British plan in favor of further study, Marshall expressed his apprehension that the cost of the British plan "had been assessed too low since the wish might have been the father to the thought." He pointedly remarked that once the "momentum" of the contemplated Mediterranean operations was started, it "would be difficult to check.[42]

The Combined Chiefs reconvened on the following day, May 19, 1943 for three separate meetings. In the first of these, held at 10:30 in the morning, they discussed in detail the separate papers prepared by the British and American planning staffs.[43] This meeting was one of unique importance, not only regarding HUSKY, but for the entire subsequent course of the Allied war effort. It was marked by great intensity on both sides.

Admiral Leahy began the proceedings by asking for the comments of the British Chiefs on the substance of the paper submitted by the United States planners. Brooke spoke for the British Chiefs. He prefaced his remarks by saying that a consideration of the papers offered by both sides showed that there was agreement among the parties on certain basic points, but that as to certain others there were "differences of opinion which must be eliminated." After briefly discussing the target date for cross-Channel operations, during which he suggested that the previously selected date of April 1, 1944 be moved back to May 1 or June 1, he moved on to the more divisive question of Italy. He pointed out that while the American paper accepted the elimination of Italy as a possibility, it had given no appreciation to the steps necessary to either accomplish it or take advantage of it. Of far greater importance, however, was the fact that the American paper contemplated a period of six to seven months following HUSKY during which Allied forces would be essentially inactive on land. This was clearly intolerable for Brooke, since in his view 1943 was "most critical" for Russia. The western

40  *F.R.U.S., Conferences at Washington and Quebec 1943.* "Meeting of the Combined Chiefs of Staff, May 18, 1943, 10:30 AM, Board of Governors Room, Federal Reserve Building," pp. 97-108.

41  *Ibid.*, p. 101.

42  *Ibid.*, pp. 101-102.

43  *F.R.U.S., Conferences at Washington and Quebec 1943.* "Meeting of the Combined Chiefs of Staff, May 19, 1943, 10:30 AM, Board of Governors Room, Federal Reserve Building," pp. 111-117.

Allies, he said, must do everything in their power to help Russia, and a failure to use all available forces for this purpose could not be justified. [44]

Brooke deftly tied together the Mediterranean operation, Germany's eastern front, and the cross-Channel attack. He said that the Allies could, with the forces then available in the Mediterranean, "achieve important results," give a great deal of aid to Russia, and at the same time create a situation that would favor an invasion of northwestern Europe in 1944. In this context, he offered a sharp but subtle criticism of the American plan. He implied that the American plan was so vague as to make it "difficult... to visualize the shape of operations to defeat Germany." However, he said that the plan "appeared" to contemplate the capture of such European ports as would permit a build-up of forces directly from the United States. A study of this concept had shown, however, that most of the capacity of such ports would be used up in supplying the forces necessary to cover them. Using Cherbourg as an example, Brooke said that provisioning the troops necessary to cover this port would be difficult unless the Germans were very weak or could not locate reserves. To this end, active Russian operations would be imperative. On the other hand, if the Russians suffered defeats in 1943, the possibility of *any* landing in Europe in the following year would be sharply reduced. This could be avoided by employing limited forces in the Mediterranean for the purpose of forcing Italy out of the war, an event which would tie up an estimated 20 to 30 German divisions. [45]

Brooke's remarks provoked a prolonged discourse by General Marshall in which he offered a pointed and detailed critique of the British plan. He commented, first of all, that the British view of port capacities was pessimistic, saying that experience had shown that estimates of such capacities should in fact be doubled. Speaking more generally of the British plan, he suggested that while it magnified the intended results of Mediterranean operations, it also minimized the forces that would be required as well as the logistic difficulties that would be encountered. The British plan was overly optimistic regarding the effect that enemy resistance would have on the operation. Marshall reminded his audience that a relatively small German force had seriously delayed Allied operations in North Africa, and said that a similar German involvement in support of Italy "might make intended operations extremely difficult and time consuming." [46]

Marshall then addressed the British plan paragraph by paragraph. He said that paragraph 2a of the plan expressed the view that it would be essential for the cross-Channel invasion to be of sufficiently large scale as would allow the pace of the Allied build-up to compete with that of the Germans. In this connection, a deteriorating situation for the Germans had been taken as a given. According to Marshall, however, the initial aim of the invasion must be not the immediate defeat of the German Army, but instead the establishment of a bridgehead that would not only affect the enemy psychologically, but also cripple the U-boat campaign and provide airfields on the Continent. This, in turn, would give the Allies better bases for operations against the Germans, thus facilitating the destruction of the *Luftwaffe*. These were immediate and important results, said Marshall, and should be regarded as the Allies' first objective, rather than an immediate advance on the Rhine. The British plan, he suggested, did not give sufficient recognition to the devastating effect that the Allied air offensive was having on Germany's overall war-fighting capacity, as well as her ability to rapidly build up forces in western Europe. [47]

General Marshall pressed home his attack. While paragraph 7 of the British paper addressed the limitations that the shortage of landing craft would force on cross-Channel operations, it failed to point out that the contemplated Mediterranean operations would further reduce the number of these all-important vehicles. Paragraph 27 asserted that the oil fields in Ploesti could not be attacked except from bases in Italy. In fact, Marshall pointed out, the Chiefs had already discussed this issue and decided that bases already in Allied hands would be sufficient for the mounting of such an attack. Paragraph 35 overestimated the willingness of the Italian people to deal with the Allies. A more likely course of events, Marshall suggested, was that Germany would support the Italians to the fullest extent possible, Allied plans would be seriously delayed, the Mediterranean theatre would siphon off Allied resources, "and we should find ourselves completely involved in operations in that theatre to the exclusion of all else." [48]

Marshall turned to paragraph 38 of the British plan, which proposed that the Allies should secure a bridgehead at Durazzo in the event that Italy collapsed. Such an operation, in Marshall's view, would so completely commit the Allies that subsequent operations of any significance would be rendered impossible as a result of shipping and landing craft shortages. Marshall stated that the summary of troop

[44] *Ibid.*, pp. 112-113.
[45] *Ibid.*, p. 113.
[46] *Ibid.*

[47] *Ibid.*, pp. 114-115.
[48] *Ibid.*, p. 115.

commitments set forth in paragraph 42 of the British plan might well be an accurate estimate. It was "axiomatic," however, that all military commanders invariably asked for more troops than had originally been estimated as sufficient. The proposed Mediterranean operations would be no different, and Allied commanders would soon be "overwhelmed" by demands for more troops and equipment. The same was true of British estimates concerning the shipping requirements necessary to support the Italian economy in the event of that country's collapse. While the British had contemplated a maximum of 20 ships per month would be required for this task, it was more likely that twice this number would be needed.[49]

Marshall also complained that the British plan had underestimated the number of ships that would be required for the build-up of troops in the United Kingdom for the cross-Channel attack. If operations in the Mediterranean continued after HUSKY, the pre-invasion build-up in England would be curtailed by a lack of sufficient escorts, even if enough troop and cargo ships were available. And if the Allies mounted significant operations in the Mediterranean after HUSKY, there would be no landing craft returned to England for use in the invasion of the Continent. Marshall concluded by saying that in general the British plan was too pessimistic concerning the possibilities for successful cross-Channel operations, since it failed to take into account the success of the Allied air offensive and its relationship to the ground campaign. The British view of Mediterranean operations, on the other hand, was overly optimistic in its assessment of the forces which would be required, the strength of the enemy reaction and the magnitude of the logistic problem.[50]

At this point the discussion became so heated that Marshall suggested that it continue "off the record." As a result, all of the officers present, with the exception of the Combined Chiefs of Staff themselves, withdrew from the meeting. Brooke, though not altogether satisfied with the agreement ultimately reached during this closed-door session, later said that it was "far better than a break-up of the Conference."[51]

Unenthusiastic as the British Chiefs may have been about the end result, it was their point of view which carried the day. The contentious meetings of the Combined Chiefs produced a report, entitled "TRIDENT: Report to the President and Prime Minister of the Final Agreed Summary of Conclusions Reached by the Combined Chiefs of Staff," which they presented in final form to Roosevelt and Churchill on May 25, 1943.[52] The report enunciated the overall strategic objective of the Allies to be "the unconditional surrender of the Axis powers."[53] Among the specific operations planned for 1943-1944 to achieve this purpose were "Operations in the Mediterranean to Eliminate Italy from the War." On this point, the report stated that the Combined chiefs had resolved to direct General Eisenhower

> ... as a matter of urgency, to plan such operations in exploitation of HUSKY as are best calculated to eliminate Italy from the War and to contain the maximum number of German forces. Which of the various specific operations should be adopted, and thereafter mounted, is a decision which will be reserved to the Combined Chiefs of Staff.

The report allocated to Eisenhower 27 divisions (19 British and Allied, 4 United States and 4 French) for post-HUSKY operations in the Mediterranean. This was the entire complement of Allied forces then available in the theatre, with the exception of 4 American and 3 British divisions, which were to be withdrawn to the United Kingdom for use in cross-Channel operations, and 2 British divisions, which represented the British commitment to Turkey. In addition, the report assigned to Eisenhower's command over 3,600 aircraft, including over 1,000 bombers of all types and approximately 2,000 fighters.[54]

At the operational level, General Eisenhower and his planning staff also confronted the question of how to proceed against Italy following the conclusion of the Sicilian campaign. In late April, the A.F.H.Q. planners advocated the very scheme that was anathema to Churchill, namely the seizure of Sardinia and Corsica, followed by a bombing offensive against the Italian mainland from bases on these islands and Sicily. The purpose of this air assault would be to drive Italy from the war, or in the alternative to lay the groundwork for an amphibious invasion. The planners gave no consideration to the notion of invading Italy from Sicily without the intermediate step of conquering Sardinia and Corsica.[55]

---

49  *Ibid.*, pp. 115-116.
50  *Ibid.*, p. 116.
51  *Ibid.*, n. 7.

52  *F.R.U.S., Conferences at Washington and Quebec 1943,* "Report of the Combined Chiefs of Staff to President Roosevelt and Prime Minister Churchill, pp. 364-373.
53  *Ibid.*, p. 365.
54  *Ibid.*, p. 368.
55  Albert N. Garland and Howard M. Smyth, *United States Army in World War II; The Mediterranean Theater of Operations; Sicily and the Surrender of Italy,* Center of Military History, United States Army, Washington, D.C. 1986, p. 14.

While Eisenhower could do little else but side with his planners generally on the subject of the practical aspects of prosecuting the war in the Mediterranean, he was nevertheless convinced that the best strategy for the Allies was a cross-Channel invasion directed at Germany through northern France. Thus, although he considered with Marshall a variety of scenarios, ultimately Eisenhower favored bringing an end to further offensive action in the Mediterranean, if those operations might be expected to interfere with the build-up for the invasion of France. In this Eisenhower was in fact supported by his planners, who saw the proposed operation against Sardinia and Corsica in a favorable light because they would require limited troop commitments, and would allow the Allies the opportunity to move away from Italy if they so desired.[56]

The point of view advocated by Eisenhower and the American planners was not shared by their English colleagues. Tedder, for example, believed that the Sardinian operation would be more costly than expected, and that it would not yield the kind of air bases that would be of particular use against the Reich. Indeed, he and his associates on the British planning staff did not think in terms of the cross-Channel operation as the ultimate goal of Allied European strategy. Instead, they favored the large scale employment of air power, much of it based in central Italy, along with the steady erosion of German fighting power, to be obtained not only by bombing but also through direct and indirect application of force in the Balkans. The British saw the key to Allied victory in the removal of Italy from the war, rather than the cross-Channel invasion of Europe.[57]

The British planners recommended invading the toe of Italy if Italy did not sue for peace during HUSKY. They did not see the successful seizure of Corsica and Sardinia as necessary prerequisites for this. Their view was that operations on the Italian mainland would be more likely to lead to the collapse of Italy in 1943, and that this would open a land front capable of attracting and holding a large number of Axis forces. For this purpose, they advocated invading the toe of Italy before completion of the Sicilian campaign. This would achieve the most immediate goal, namely the withdrawal of Italy from the war.[58]

Churchill was not comfortable with the failure of the combined Chiefs of Staff to conclude the TRIDENT conference with an explicit call for the invasion of Italy in 1943. He therefore flew to Algiers to visit Eisenhower, taking General Marshall, General Brooke and the Prime Minister's personal Chief of Staff, General Sir Hastings L. Ismay, in tow. Churchill's purpose was to persuade Eisenhower and his planners to select the Italian mainland, rather than Corsica and Sardinia, as the target of invasion.[59]

Churchill convened a formal meeting to address his concerns on May 29, 1943. The officers present included Eisenhower, Marshall and Walter Bedell Smith on the American side, and Brooke, Alexander, Cunningham and Tedder on the British. Marshall took the initiative, urging that Eisenhower establish two wholly independent and fully staffed headquarters. They would be tasked to prepare operational plans for the invasion of the Italian mainland and Corsica/Sardinia respectively. When the situation in Sicily allowed, one of these headquarters would be given the authority and the necessary resources to take action. The parties then discussed the variety of possibilities that the Sicilian operation might hold, as well as the uncertainties presented by the lack of solid information concerning the respective attitudes of the Italians and Germans about the coming fight. There was general agreement, including even by Churchill, that the Italian mainland should not be invaded in the face of strong resistance. Ultimately, Marshall's concept of dual headquarters prevailed at this conference. In effect, Churchill's anxiety for a timely invasion of Italy gave way in the face of situational logic. General Eisenhower, the man who would likely lead such an invasion, demonstrated that under the circumstances there were only three likely scenarios involving Italy, namely: (1) an immediate collapse of enemy resistance on Sicily, in which event the Allies should shift the assault to the mainland with dispatch; (2) stubborn and prolonged enemy resistance on Sicily, a development that would result in no Allied forces being available for an operation against Italy any time soon; and (3) strong enemy resistance on Sicily nevertheless overcome by the Allies with relative speed, a situation whose details were so unpredictable that no advance planning could be made. Even Churchill was compelled to recognize that of these three alternatives only the first offered the possibility of a quick Allied initiative against the Italian mainland, and that possibility was slim at best, given the presence of German units on the island.[60]

## ALLIED AND AXIS PLANS AND DISPOSITIONS

On June 7, 1943 Eisenhower outlined his plan for the invasion of Sicily to the War Department. In addition to the elaborate air plan, which called upon each of

---

[56] *Ibid.*
[57] *Ibid.*, p. 15.
[58] *Ibid.*, p. 16.

[59] *Ibid.*, p. 23.
[60] *Ibid.*, p. 24.

the various air commands in the Mediterranean area to contribute to either the build-up or the invasion itself, Eisenhower described a series of simultaneous seaborne assaults, assisted by air landings, to capture the seaports of Licata and Syracuse and the airfields between these cities, in order to lay the groundwork for operations against the airfields at Gerbini, Catania and Augusta. Patton's Seventh Army would be aboard the ships of the Western Naval Task Force, commanded by U.S. Admiral Hewitt, while the Eastern Naval Task Force, commanded by British Admiral Bertram Ramsay, would convey Montgomery's Eighth Army. The latter was to operate in the eastern sector, and had as its objectives the port of Syracuse and the airfield at Pachino. Its XIII Corps was to land south of Cap Murro Di Porco with 5th Division on a two-brigade front, 50th Division on a one-brigade front and 3d Commando. XXX Corps would operate on three sides of Passero, where the 231st Brigade, 51st Division would advance on a one brigade front, while Canadian 1st Division would do so on a two brigade front, next to the 40th and 41st Royal Marine Commandos. XIII Corps was to move on to the port and airfield at Augusta, thence to the airfields at Catania and Gerbini. XXX Corps would effect a junction with the right flank of U.S. Seventh Army. This American force was to land at Cap Scalambri, Scoglitti, Gela and Licata. II U.S. Corps, comprising the 1st Infantry Division and 45th Infantry Division, would take the fields at Biscari, Ponte Olivo, Gela and Comiso. At the same time, 3d Infantry Division and an armored Combat Command from 2d Armored Division would capture the port and airfield at Licata, the rest of the 2d Armored Division remaining in reserve. Admiral Hewitt later reported that the placing of the 1st Infantry Division and 45th Infantry Division (corresponding to CENT and DIME landing forces respectively) under II U.S. Corps command created "many difficulties." He believed that it was neither desirable nor feasible to place the CENT and DIME naval forces under one command. For one thing, the CENT transports arrived in the theatre from the United States under naval command. The overlay of the Army Corps command had no naval equivalent, thus causing needless conflict. There was also trouble with the echelon of the air command for the campaign. While an air officer on the same echelon as the Naval Commander, Western Naval Task Force, and Commanding General, Seventh Army, was established, the air officer lacked authority to order aircraft into the assault area. The naval and army officers in question also lacked authority to direct the use of aircraft to support the assault force. This command arrangement was "not conducive to suc-cess."

There had been a plan to use the available airborne troops to neutralize the beach defenses, but this notion was abandoned in the final plan. Under the revised scheme, the British 1st Airborne Division was to drop by parachute and glider in the area south of Syracuse to seize important tactical targets, while four battalions of the U.S. 82d Airborne Division dropped in the area behind Gela. Staging for the invasion was a most complex affair; for example, British and Canadian troops were to come from the United Kingdom, the Middle East and Tunisia, while their American allies came not only from nearby North Africa, but in the case of the 45th Infantry Division, directly from the United States as well. As a result, many of the assaulting units were required to bring with them at least 21 days maintenance, with an additional 7 days maintenance in reserve. All of this, of course, placed a tremendous strain on Allied shipping.

Because the new plan abandoned the concept of seizing the port of Palermo, FORCE 343, or U.S. Seventh Army was denied a useful harbor. This meant, in turn, that this force had to plan on being supplied over the beach until at least D plus 30. Since the first convoy from the United States was not scheduled to arrive in Sicily before D plus 14, special measures had to be taken to ensure continuous supply of the fighting troops. These included an arrangement with FORCE 545 (British Eighth Army) for the partial use of Syracuse after D plus 14. In addition, 2500 service troops were detailed to Syracuse, and special depots were established near the town, all for the purpose of supplying FORCE 343 prior to the arrival of the first convoy from the United States.

The total number of vessels in the combined Allied naval forces exceeded 3200; 1700 were assigned to the Western Naval Task Force, and the remainder to its eastern counterpart. Two thousand of these boats and ships were to participate in the initial assault. In protecting this fleet, Eisenhower and his staff were concerned not only with the Axis air forces, but also with the potential threat posed by the Italian Navy. In view of the consistent failure of this force to successfully engage the Royal Navy, the Allied commanders rated it low in morale and tactical ability. Nevertheless, it could not be ignored, possessing as it did six battleships and two cruisers, and the view was that if it were ever to stand and fight, this would be the occasion. The Allied force deployed to counter the threat of the Italian Navy was a formidable one, comprising the First Battle Squadron of the Royal Navy in the Mediterranean. This consisted of two commands, FORCE H, including the battleships

*Warspite, Valiant, Nelson* and *Rodney*, and the aircraft carriers *Indomitable* and *Formidable*, and FORCE Z, with the battleships *King George V* and *Howe*. On D minus 1, FORCE H was to move into the Ionian Sea in such a way as to appear to threaten the west coast of Greece on D Day, thus serving as a means to divert the enemy's attention at the critical moment, and it was to maintain this position until D plus 2. Both FORCE H and FORCE Z were, of course, to be available to intervene against the Italian Navy should it put in an appearance, as well as to offer fire support to the invasion force, should the need arise. In the event, neither such contingency transpired. In addition to the British First Battle Squadron, the Western and Eastern Naval Task Forces boasted eight cruisers and eight destroyers for use in a fire support role, as well as seven Royal Navy submarines—*Safari, Shakespeare, Seraph, Unruffled, Unseen, Unison, Unrivalled*—serving as beacons off the coast of Sicily.

The Allied cover plan provided for false D-day and false destinations for the assault force, and the movement of the assault convoys was designed to further this deception by being scheduled for the routes of normal through convoys. By these means did the Allies intend for the Axis to be forced to contend with at least two other threatened invasions, one in the Balkans and the other in southern France. Thus, as FORCE H maneuvered in the Ionian Sea for the apparent invasion of Greece, so also would the Allied convoys, moving in their accustomed routes, converge south of Malta to suggest a threat to Crete. Behind these deceptions lay the Allied fear of the Germans, and in particular their fear that the Germans would reinforce Sicily ahead of the scheduled invasion.

The Allied target date of July 10 was in part based on an assumption that the Tunisian campaign would be concluded by April 30. In the event, this did not occur until May 13, a circumstance which caused Eisenhower and his staff considerable concern about whether the assault would take place in a timely fashion. To some degree, this concern was caused by the fact that the Allied forces involved needed, but lacked, adequate training in combined operations. A combined training center was established at the Algerian port of Djidjelli. From here the British 51st Division and 78th Division were able to participate in combined training; three complete naval rehearsals and one combined rehearsal were carried out with these forces, the only elements in the Eastern Task Force to be involved in such full rehearsals. Other components of the Eastern Task Force were not so fortunate; the Canadian 1st Division trained in the United Kingdom, while the British 5th Division and

50th Division and the 231st Brigade trained in the Middle East, where a shortage of landing craft restricted training to the desert, with the exception of several "incomplete" landing rehearsals in the Gulf of Aqaba.

U.S. forces had the benefit of six bases in Algeria, as well as two in Tunisia. The U.S. 3d Infantry Division trained in Tunisia, while the 1st Infantry Division and the 2d Armored Division underwent amphibious training in Algeria. On June 22 the 45th Infantry Division arrived in combat loaders directly from the United States. Its elements disembarked at Oran. The 1st, 3d and 45th Infantry Divisions were able to undergo some rehearsals, but Eisenhower referred to them as dry runs on a reduced scale. They involved landing only selected units of each Regimental Combat Team on the rehearsal beaches, with the result that there was no complete unloading of even a limited number of ships and craft. As a result, these rehearsals stopped short of what Eisenhower called the "critical phase," in which beaches become crowded and disorganized through the accretion of supplies and disabled boats and other equipment. These exercises had to suffice, however, because of the immediate presence of Axis aircraft and submarines.

The Allied rehearsals were complete by July 4. Thereafter, vehicles used in them had been returned to concentration areas for re-waterproofing and re-loading aboard ship. The troops were returned to their final staging areas. The 82d Airborne Division arrived in Tunisia from Casablanca. The port of Bizerte was choked with 15 days reserve supplies for 140,000 men, three and a half units of fire, and replacements for 25% of the combat vehicles, 10% of the general purpose vehicles, and 10% of the weapons.

During the period immediately before the landings in Sicily, the Allied air forces at Malta were dramatically increased in size, from 200 first line aircraft in November 1942 to over 600 in June, 1943. These were operating from enlarged and newly constructed airfields, from which Mosquitoes and Spitfires harried the enemy on Sicily during June. Added to these forces were an additional 70 aircraft based on Gozo and Pantelleria (following its liberation). There was, in fact, an excess of aircraft available to the Allies, although the same was not true with respect to the available fuel and ordinance. Indeed the air campaign against Pantelleria consumed so much in the way of necessary bombs and gasoline that only just sufficient supplies of these materials were available for the Sicilian operation.

From June 11 to July 10, 1943 the primary target for the Allied air forces was the system of Axis air bases on Sicily and Sardinia. In the previous three months the number of bases available to the enemy had increased from 19 to over 30 on Sicily alone, so that approximately 600 fighter aircraft could be accommodated. The Allied air assault on these bases began on June 12, the Sicilian bases being attacked repeatedly until June 30. The Allies also attacked the Sardinian bases, beginning on June 28. These raids were not heavily contested by the enemy, who lost a good number of fighters on the ground, and transferred still others to bases thought to be more secure, namely those in the eastern part of Sicily. During the last week before the invasion the attention of the Allied air forces turned to these bases as well. The result was that by July 10, the enemy had virtually no fully serviceable airfields on the island, and indeed most of its bases had been rendered totally useless.

Meanwhile, the Allied air forces had also been attacking the enemy's communications centers in Naples, as well as Messina, and the Sardinian ports at Olbia and Golfo Aranci. The Allies struck Naples and its neighboring rail junction four times during June. The Sardinian ports suffered a like number of air strikes during the same period. Messina received particular attention. During the weeks immediately preceding the invasion, the Allies bombed it seven times, including three raids on successive nights during which the ferry facilities on both side of the Straits were thoroughly blasted. Finally, during the night of July 9-10, the Allied air forces delivered large scale attacks on what remained of the enemy's air bases in Sicily, as well as upon the assault areas themselves.

One gains a general appreciation of the context in which *HUSKY* occurred by first considering the relative position of the island of Sicily in its Mediterranean setting. Sicily is generally triangular in shape. It is oriented along a roughly east/west axis, and its base extends from north to south between Messina and Cape Passero. The southern side of the island stretches from the Cape to Marsala, while the equally lengthy northern side reaches from Messina to Trapani.

An exceedingly narrow body of water, the Straits of Messina, separates Sicily from the Italian mainland. The area thus separated from Sicily is the toe of the Italian boot. The Tyrrhenian Sea to the north divides the island from Sardinia, Corsica and the principal cities of Italy, such as Rome and Naples. The Mediterranean to the south and east creates a substantial barrier between Sicily and its neighbors in North Africa, Tunisia, Tripolitania and Cyrenaica. Of particular significance for the coming battle were the islands of Pantelleria, nearly equidistant between Sicily and

the northeastern coast of Tunisia, and Malta, situated almost directly south of Cape Passero by a relatively few air miles.

Sicily enjoys rather hot summers and mild winters. In July, when the Allied invasion came, the normal temperature range is between 70 and 90 degrees Fahrenheit. Rainfall is moderate at best, averaging between 10 and 20 inches from the first of May to the end of October. In July, Sicily is typically in a boundary zone between a high pressure zone that prevails over the Atlantic Ocean and a low pressure zone that covers the whole of the Eurasian land mass and North Africa. The planners of the invasion, and those who would fight in it, could therefore expect hot and dry weather, which nevertheless might be interrupted by storms of some severity.

Sicily is part of the Alpine system which predominates throughout southern Europe, northern Africa and northern Turkey. Mountainous terrain extends generally from the center of the island to the coasts. In the north, the hills virtually touch the coast, while in the south a narrow strip of flat ground lies between the sea and the mountains. The approaches to Messina are protected in the west by the Caronie Mountains. Along the eastern coast, south of Messina and immediately north of Catania, lies Mount Etna, the most dominant topographical feature on the island.

Apart from the southern coastal strip, there are three relatively flat areas on the island of sufficient breadth and depth to allow an invading force to land, deploy and move inland. The first of these, at the western end of Sicily, extends from Trapani to Mazara, thus embracing the entire tip of the island. At its midpoint, this coastal plain is approximately twenty miles deep, from Marsala at the water's edge where the mountainous terrain begins. Inviting as this potential landing ground is, however, the Allies eventually elected not to land a single soldier there. This was in part due to the fact that several enemy formations were stationed directly behind the potential landing zones. More importantly, the more substantial Axis units were located at the eastern end of Sicily. To engage these troops from the west would require traversing virtually the entire length of the island.

In the middle of the eastern end of Sicily, beginning in the foothills of Mount Etna and reaching southward along the coast to Augusta, lies the Plain of Catania. It is roughly twenty miles deep and twenty miles wide, although deeper and wider than this in certain places. To the southeast of this plain, and separated from it by a chain of hills, is another coastal plain, reaching from Licata in the west around the southeast tip of the island to Syracuse. The two deepest portions of this plain, between Gela and Scoglitti on the south coast, and at Cape Passero on the southeastern tip, are both approximately fifteen miles in depth. In the event, the main force of the Allied blow fell in these two areas.

The Axis forces committed to defend Sicily included a variety of German and Italian troops, some of whom were stationed on the island on July 10, 1943, and some of whom were shifted to the island as the battles progressed. All Axis forces on the island operated under the direction of Armed Forces Command Sicily, commanded by Generale d'Armata Alfredo Guzzoni. This headquarters had a German liaison office attached to it, under the able *General* Ferdinand von Senger und Etterlin, as well as German naval and Luftwaffe headquarters. Tactical control of all Axis units on Sicily, both Italian and German, resided with Sixth Italian Army, also under the command of Guzzoni. The headquarters subordinate to Sixth Italian Army included XII Corps (Italian) and XVI Corps (Italian); the anti-aircraft defense command for Sicily; the separate and independent Italian Navy and Royal Italian Air Force commands for Italy; and the XIV *Panzer Korps*, under *General der Panzertruppen* Hans Valentin Hube.[61]

The major German units to fight in Sicily were *15. Panzer-Grenadier-Division, Hermann Göring Panzer-Division, 29. Panzer-Grenadier-Division* and *1. Fallschirm-jäger-Division*. When the Allied onslaught came, *15. Panzer-Grenadier- Division* was a unit in transition. Indeed, this formation, commanded by *Generalmajor* Eberhard Rodt, actually took its final shape during the battle. Its initial parts included the remnants of *15. Panzer-Division*, which the Allies had destroyed in Tunisia two months earlier and *Division "Sizilien,"* a collection of miscellaneous units cobbled together by the Germans on the island, principally replacement units originally intended for Tunisia, along with *Panzer-Abteilung 215*.[62]

The nominal order of battle of a *Panzer-Grenadier Division* in 1943 included two *Panzer-Grenadier* regiments, each of three battalions, and including a self-propelled *flak* company, a motorized infantry gun company and a motorized engineer company; an armored battalion, in which assault guns (a total of 42) frequently substituted for tanks; an armored reconnaissance battalion, a motorized artillery regiment, a motorized tank-destroyer battalion, an anti-aircraft battalion and an engineer battalion.[63]

The makeup of *15. Panzer-Grenadier-Division* on July 10, 1943 was typical of many German formations at this stage of the war, in that it varied substantially from the prescribed establishment. *Panzer-Grenadier-Regiment 104* deployed three rifle battalions of three companies each, one heavy weapons company, one anti-tank company, and an infantry gun company. *Panzer-Grenadier-Regiment 129* and *Panzer-Grenadier-Regiment 115* were organized like their sister regiment. The Division also included *Panzer-Grenadier-Bataillon Reggio, Panzer-Abteilung 215, Artillerie-Regiment 33, Flak-Bataillon 315, Pioneer-Abteilung 33*, service troops and a *panzerjäger* battalion. *Panzer-Abteilung 215* was composed of three companies with a total of six *Panzer Mk III* and 46 *Panzer Mk IV* tanks.[64]

*29. Panzer-Grenadier-Division* also differed from the nominal establishment of such a formation. On Sicily, this division included *Panzer-Grenadier-Regiments 15* and *71*, each of three battalions; *Panzer-Abteilung 129*, which sent 43 *Stug III* assault guns to the island; *Artillerie-Regiment 29*, which possessed three battalions of self-propelled guns; and *Flak-Bataillon 313*.[65]

*Generalmajor* Walter Fries commanded *29. Panzer-Grenadier-Division* at the time of the Allied assault. The division had come into existence in 1936. It became a motorized formation in the autumn of 1937, after which it was designated *29. Infanterie-Division (Mot.)*. It distinguished itself both in Poland and in France during the race for the English Channel. In June, 1941, the division began its service in Russia with Army Group Center. It fought in several major engagements in that year, at Bialystok and Minsk, at the Dnieper crossings, and at Smolensk. The following year, it served again the German campaign in South Russia, fighting at Kharkov and in the Don bend. It was part of the assault force at Stalingrad, where it was encircled and destroyed in January, 1943.[66]

61  Carlo D'Este, *Bitter Victory: The Battle for Sicily, 1943*, New York, N.Y., 1988, p. 600.

62  Samuel W. Mitcham, Jr., *Hitler's Legions: The German Army Order of Battle, World War II*, p. 399.

63  Bryan Perrett, *Knights of the Black Cross: Hitler's Panzerwaffe and its Leaders*, London, 1986, p. 245; W.J.K. Davies, *German Army Handbook, 1939-1945*, New York, N.Y. 1973, p. 35; George F. Nafziger, *The German Order of Battle: Panzers and Artillery in World War II*, Mechanicsburg, Pa. 1999, p. 319.

64  D'Este, *Bitter Victory*, pp. 601-602; Nafziger, *Panzers and Artillery in World War II*, p. 269; Thomas L. Jentz, ed., *Panzertruppen: The Complete Guide to the Creation and Combat Employment of Germany's Tank Force 1943-1945*, Atglen, Pa., 1996, p. 103; G. Tessin, *Verbande und Truppen der deutschen Wehrmacht und Waffen SS 1939-1945*, v. 4, pp. 9-11.

65  Tessin, v. 4, pp. 273-274; Nafziger, *Panzers and Artillery in World War II*, p. 284; Jentz, p. 103.

66  Tessin, v. 4, p. 273.

The *29. Panzer-Grenadier-Division* that fought in Sicily was reconstituted in southern France the following spring. Its core formation was *345. Infanterie-Division (Mot.)*. *Generalmajor* Fries was a well-decorated officer, holding the Knights Cross with Oak Leaves and Swords, and had formerly commanded *Infanterie-Regiment (Mot.)15.* of *29. Infanterie-Division (Mot.)* during 1941-1942.[67]

In general, the establishment of a panzer division in 1943 included a panzer regiment of two battalions. In theory, the first battalion was to have four companies of 22 *Panther* tanks each; the second battalion was to have the same organization, but with *Panzer IV*s. The divisional establishment also had two motorized infantry regiments, each having two battalions. There were also a motorized artillery regiment, having three battalions; an armored reconnaissance battalion; a tank-destroyer battalion; an anti-aircraft battalion and an engineer battalion.[68]

*Panzer-Division "Hermann Göring"* that fought in Sicily under the command of *Generalleutnant* Paul Conrath exceeded in strength the accepted establishment for a panzer division. It was composed of *Panzer-Regiment "Hermann Göring"* (three battalions); *Panzer-Grenadier-Regiment 1 "Hermann Göring"* (two battalions); *Panzer-Grenadier-Regiment 2 "Hermann Göring"* (two battalions); *Panzer-Artillerie-Regiment "Hermann Göring"* (three battalions); *Flak-Regiment "Hermann Göring"*; *Panzer-Aufklarungs-Abteilung "Hermann Göring"*; and *Panzer-Pioneer-Bataillon "Hermann Göring."* The establishment of the *Panzer-Division "Hermann Göring"* exceeded the norm in that its panzer regiment had three battalions, and it fielded an anti-aircraft regiment rather than just a battalion.[69]

On Sicily, *Panzer-Regiment "Hermann Göring"* fielded two tank battalions, totaling 43 *Panzer III*s mounting long 50mm guns, three *Panzer III*s with 75mm guns and 32 *Panzer IV*s with long 75mm guns, and a battalion of 29 assault guns. Its *Panzer-Aufklarungs-Abteilung "Hermann Göring"* and *Panzer-Pioneer-Bataillon "Hermann Göring"* both fought as motorized infantry. Its *Panzer-Artillerie-Regiment "Hermann Göring"* committed only three of its four battalions, one light battalion of two batteries, and two medium battalions, each having two medium field howitzer batteries and one battery of 100 mm. guns. In addition, its *Flak-Regiment "Hermann Göring"* was under strength, fielding only one mixed battalion of three medium and three light batteries.

Finally, both of the division's *panzergrenadier* regiments fought on Sicily; however, while both battalions of *Panzer-Grenadier-Regiment 2* saw action, only the first battalion of *Panzer-Grenadier-Regiment 1* accompanied it, and all three units operated under the command of *Panzer-Grenadier-Regiment 1.*[70]

*Fallschirm-Jaeger-Division*, which was to serve with great distinction in Sicily and elsewhere, was nominally composed of *Fallschirm-Jaeger-Regiments 1, 3 and 4, Fallschirm-Artillerie-Regiment 1, Fallschirm-Flak-Abteilung 1, Fallschirm-Panzerjäger-Batallion 1, Fallschirm-Pioneer-Bataillon 1* and a signal battalion. Not all of this force, however, joined in the battle. Absent were *Fallschirm-Jaeger-Regiment 1, Fallschirm-Flak-Abteilung 1*, all but one battalion of *Fallschirm-Artillerie-Regiment* and most of the anti-tank and signal battalions.[71]

The officer commanding *1 Fallschirm-Jaeger-Division* in Sicily was *Generalleutnant* Richard Heidrich, an officer decorated with the Knight's Cross with Oak Leaves and Swords. Heidrich had previously commanded *Fallschirm-Jaeger-Regiment* of *7. Flieger-Division*, the unit from which *1. Fallschirm-Jaeger-Division* was formed in Russia in the fall of 1942. He was well-experienced, having served in the invasion of France, the airborne assault on Crete and at the siege of Leningrad. Heidrich withdrew *1 Fallschirm-Jaeger-Division* from Russia in early spring, 1943, taking it to southern France to complete its fitting and training.[72]

Also present on Sicily, and assigned to *Panzer-Division "Hermann Göring,"* was the second company of *Schwere-Panzer-Abteilung 504*. This unit fielded 17 *Tiger* tanks, each mounting the formidable 88mm gun.[73]

Several Italian Army units defended Sicily as well. Foremost among these was 4th (Livorno) Division, commanded by Generale di Divisione Domenico Chirieleison. It was composed of 33rd and 34th Infantry Regiments, a mortar battalion, XI Commando Battalion, IV Anti-Tank Battalion, 28th Artillery Regiment, three anti-aircraft battalions and an engineer battalion. Although other Italian units on Sicily were characterized as "mobile," Livorno was in fact the only such formation on the island. It was generally superior to all other Italian formations, with troops of exceptional quality and enough of its own transport to move all of its regiments at once.[74]

67  *Ibid.*
68  Jentz, *Panzertruppen*, p. 53.
69  Tessin, v. 14, p. 117; Nafziger, *Panzers and Artillery in World War II*, pp. 175-177.

70  D'Este, *Bitter Victory*, p. 602; Jentz, *Panzertruppen*, p. 103.
71  D'Este, *Bitter Victory*, p. 605; Tessin, v.2, pp. 63-64; .
72  Mitcham, *Hitler's Legions*, p. 404;
73  Jentz, *Panzertruppen*, p. 103.
74  D'Este, *Bitter Victory*, pp. 601-602.

There were three additional "mobile" Italian formations of divisional size on Sicily. One of these was 28th (Aosta) Division, under Generale di Divisione Giacomo Romano. It fielded 5th and 6th Infantry Regiments, 171st "Blackshirt" Battalion, XXVIII Mortar Battalion, 22nd Artillery Regiment, two anti-aircraft batteries and an engineer battalion. The second was 26th (Assietta) Division, eventually commanded by General di Divisione Ottorino Schreiber. It was composed of 29th and 30th Infantry Regiments, 17th "Blackshirt" Battalion, CXXVI Mortar Battalion, 25th Artillery Regiment, two anti-aircraft batteries and an engineer battalion. The third such formation was 54th (Napoli) Division, under General di Divisione Giulio G.C. Porcinari. It included 75th and 76th Infantry Regiments, 173rd "Blackshirt" Battalion, 54th Artillery Regiment and two anti-aircraft batteries.[75]

The Italians also deployed several static coastal defense units on Sicily. XII Corps, under the command of Generale di Corpo d'Armata Mario Arisio, included 202nd, 207th and 208th Coastal Divisions, and 146th Coastal Regiment. XVI Corps, commanded by Generale di Corpo d'Armata Carlo Rossi, had 206th and 213th Coastal Divisions, as well as XVIII and XIX Coastal Brigades. These static formations were composed primarily of Sicilian conscripts in the higher age groups. The weaponry issued to these units was outdated, and consisted primarily of small arms and some low grade artillery. In addition to being poorly armed and manned, these Italian coastal defense units were assigned unreasonably large stretches of beach, so that what little strength they did have was dissipated. As a result of these deficiencies, they failed to acquit themselves well on the day of the invasion.[76]

On the eve of the invasion, the principal Axis forces on the island were roughly equally divided between the western and eastern ends, because of uncertainty about where the Allies would land. At the western end of Sicily the slightly under strength *15. Panzer-Grenadier-Division* lay between 28th (Aosta) Division on the north and 26th (Assietta) Division on the south. All three units were deployed in the hills immediately behind the coastal plain. At the island's other end, from west to east, were 4th (Livorno) Division, *Panzer-Division "Hermann Göring,"* also under strength, and 54th (Napoli) Division. *"Hermann Göring"* and 54th (Napoli) divisions were directly west of Syracuse, in the hills to the south of the plain of Catania. 4th (Livorno) Division was also in the hills, north of Licata and Gela. A smaller Axis force,

a collection of various formations known as Group Schmalz, was positioned north of the plain of Catania, at the foot of Mount Etna. *29. Panzer-Grenadier-Division* and *1. Fallschirm-Jäger-Division* were not on Sicily when the Allied assault came.[77]

The total Axis forces ultimately involved in the defense of Sicily has been variously estimated at between 270,000 and 370,000 men. Of this figure, the maximum number of German troops was about 62,000.[78] Arrayed against the island's defenders was a very considerable Allied ground force, consisting of more than two armies. While General Eisenhower led the overall operation, his ground commander was General Sir Harold R.L.G. Alexander, Commander-in-Chief, 15th Army Group. Alexander's principal subordinates were General Sir Bernard Law Montgomery, commanding Eighth Army, and Lieutenant General George S. Patton, Jr., commanding Seventh United States Army.[79]

Eighth Army's XIII Corps, under the command of Lieutenant-General Miles Dempsey, included three divisions. The first of these was 5th Division, under Major-General H.P.M. Berney-Ficklin. It was composed of 13th Infantry Brigade, 15th Infantry Brigade and 17th Infantry Brigade. 5th Division also disposed of a reconnaissance regiment, an anti-tank regiment, a light anti-aircraft regiment, three field artillery regiments and additional support units.[80]

XIII Corps' second major formation was 50th Division (Northumbrian), under Major-General Sidney C. Kirkman. This division fielded 69th Infantry Brigade, 151st Infantry Brigade and 168th Infantry Brigade. 50th Division also possessed an anti-tank regiment, a light anti-aircraft regiment and three field artillery regiments, plus additional support troops. The third division under the command of XIII Corps was 1st Airborne Division, under Major-General G.F. Hopkinson. 1st Airborne Division included 1st Parachute Brigade (three battalions), 2nd Parachute Brigade (three battalions), 4th Parachute Brigade (three battalions) and 1st Airlanding Brigade (two battalions). 1st Airborne Division fielded a reconnaissance squadron, a light artillery regiment, two anti-tank batteries, a light anti-aircraft battery and three squadrons of engineers. It also possessed a myriad signals and medical support units. Finally, XIII Corps had under its command 44th Royal Tank Regiment.[81]

The commander of XXX Corps was Lieutenant-

---

[75] *Ibid.,* pp. 603-604.
[76] *Ibid.,* pp. 602-603.

[77] Garland and Smyth, *Sicily and the Surrender of Italy,* Map 1.
[78] *Ibid.,* pp. 75-87; D'Este, *Bitter Victory,* p. 606.
[79] D'Este, *Bitter Victory,* pp. 584, 588.
[80] *Ibid.,* pp. 584-585.
[81] *Ibid.,* pp. 585-586.

General Sir Oliver Leese. First among his troops were those of 51st (Highland) Division, under Major-General Douglas Wimberley. 51st Division included 152nd, 153rd and 154th Infantry Brigades. It also had three regiments of field artillery, one regiment each of light anti-aircraft and anti-tank guns, and other support units. The other major formation under the control of XXX Corps was 1st Canadian Division, under Major-General G.G. Simonds. It had 1st, 2nd and 3d Infantry Brigades, a reconnaissance regiment, an anti-tank regiment, three regiments of field artillery and other troops, including combat engineers.[82]

In place of a third division, XXX Corps controlled three additional independent brigades. One of these was 231st Infantry Brigade, commanded by Brigadier R.E. Urquhart. This unit was composed of three battalions of infantry, a regiment of field artillery and a company of combat engineers. XXX corps controlled in addition 1st Canadian Army Tank Brigade and 23rd Armored Brigade, each of which fielded three regiments of tanks.[83]

15th Army Group also had available a substantial reserve. This included 78th Division (three infantry brigades) under Major-General V. Evelegh. This unit was comparable to its sister divisional formations, in that it too contained a reconnaissance regiment, an anti-tank regiment, three field artillery regiments, a light anti-aircraft regiment as well as additional troops, including three companies of Royal Engineers.[84] 15th Army Corps had at its disposal further independent units, such as three units of commandos.[85]

Seventh United States Army was, like its British counterpart, a most formidable formation. The Army's II Corps, under Lieutenant-General Omar N. Bradley, controlled two divisions. One of them was 1st Infantry Division, which began the invasion under Major General Terry de la Mesa Allen, later succeeded by Major General Clarence R. Huebner. It had three infantry regiments, each of which formed the core of a Regimental Combat Team (RCT). The division had four field artillery battalions, plus additional units, including an engineer battalion, a reconnaissance battalion, a medical battalion and other support troops. Also attached to the division for the landing on Sicily was 67th Armored Regiment, Darby's Rangers, composed of 1st and 4th Ranger Battalions, two additional battalions of engineers, and troops of a chemical battalion.[86]

45th Infantry Division, under the command of Major General Troy H. Middleton, was the second component of II Corps. It also had three regiments of infantry and four battalions of field artillery. The division also fielded a combat engineer battalion, a medical battalion, a mechanized reconnaissance troop and numerous other support units. 753rd Medium Tank Battalion was attached to 45th Infantry Division for the invasion.[87]

Seventh Army had an additional large and powerful force available for the invasion, known as JOSS Force. It included 3d Infantry Division under Major General Lucian K. Truscott, the core of which was composed of three infantry regiments and four battalions of field artillery. 3d Infantry Division also had an engineer battalion, a chemical mortar battalion, a medical battalion, a reconnaissance troop and numerous support and headquarters units. It also had as a floating reserve 66th Armored Regiment, 41st Armored Infantry Regiment and additional reconnaissance and field artillery units, all of which constituted Combat Command A of 2d Armored Division. In addition to all these units, the Division had attached to it combat engineer, Ranger, infantry and artillery units, plus additional headquarters units.[88]

JOSS Force also controlled Seventh Army's floating reserve. This comprised Combat Command B of the 2nd Armored Division, 9th Infantry Division, 82nd Airborne Division, 18th Infantry Regiment, 540th Engineer Shore Regiment and two anti-aircraft battalions.[89]

Eighth Army was to attack south of Syracuse along the Gulf of Noto, including both sides of Cape Passero. The Allied intention was that the Port of Syracuse would quickly be brought on line, and that the advance would proceed with alacrity, soon making available the harbors at Augusta and Catania. On the other hand, the Seventh Army was to land along the gulf of Gela, roughly between that city and Licata. Although both of these towns offered modest port facilities, in fact the Americans would be compelled to rely upon supplies brought ashore through the assault beaches.

Alexander's broad concept of the battle for Sicily was that Eighth Army would dash along the coast to the Straits of Messina to deny the Axis forces an avenue of retreat, while Seventh Army advanced in parallel to protect its left flank. For this purpose, Eighth Army would land four divisions and one brigade, whose first objectives were Syracuse and a neighboring airfield. The British would drop their 1st

[82]  *Ibid.*, pp. 586-587.
[83]  *Ibid.*, p. 587.
[84]  *Ibid.*, pp. 587-588.
[85]  *Ibid.*, p. 588.
[86]  *Ibid.*, pp. 588-589.

[87]  *Ibid.*, p. 589.
[88]  *Ibid.*, p. 590.
[89]  *Ibid.*, p. 591.

Airlanding Brigade before the main body of troops arrived ashore. Its task was to seize the Ponte Grande bridge over the Anapo River near Syracuse. Preceded by a drop of a reinforced regimental combat team of the 82d Airborne Division a few miles inland of Gela, Seventh Army would place ashore three divisions between Licata and Gela.

British XIII Corps was on the north end of the British landing zone, and was to put ashore 5th Division near Cassibile and 50th Division near Avola. It also controlled British 1st Airborne Division, which was to land just south of Syracuse. This formation, along with Commando units, was to support 5th Division in seizing the port city. XIII Corps would then advance northward on Augusta and Catania.

XXX Corps would land on either side of Cape Passero. On the right, 231st Infantry Brigade was to maintain contact with XIII Corps while 51st Division secured the town of Pachino. On the left, two Royal Marine Commando units and 1st Canadian Division were to advance and make contact with Seventh Army at Ragusa. They were also to take the airfield at Pachino. 51st Division would then also begin to move northward.

Seventh Army's invasion force had two primary elements, 3d Infantry Division and II Corps. The former would land in the region of Licata, while the latter, including 1st Infantry Division and 45th Infantry Division, would attack on about sixty miles of beach to the east. Patton's reserve was divided into four main elements, namely 2d Armored Division, reinforced with a regimental combat team from 1st Infantry Division; that portion of 82d Airborne Division not involved in the air drop; a regimental combat team from 9th Infantry Division, plus that division's artillery; and the balance of 9th Infantry Division.

The final operational plan required Patton to capture the airfields at Licata, Ponte Olivo, Biscari and Comiso. He was assigned to take and restore to operation the ports of Licata and Gela. To accomplish these tasks, Patton intended to land simultaneously at Scoglitti, Licata and Gela for the purpose of securing, by the end of D plus 2, the ports of Licata and Gela, an air landing ground at Farello, and the airfields.

Third Infantry Division constituted the left side of Patton's invasion force. This division, reinforced by Combat Command A of the 2d Armored Division and a battalion of French colonial troops, the 4th Moroccan Tabor of Goums, totaled about 45,000 men. The division was to attack on four beaches, two each on either side of Licata, to seize the city, its port and the airfield. Since the division was on the far left flank of Seventh Army, with the task of protecting

that flank, its first important objective was to capture Campobello and Palma di Montechiaro. These inland cities controlled avenues of approach from the northwest, and getting at them would require the division to overcome significant natural obstacles.

In the landing zone of II Corps, 45th Infantry Division was to land on the right, and 1st Infantry Division on the left. First Infantry Division's area of operations extended from a point midway between Licata and Gela eastward to the Acate River. In addition to its small port, Gela was noteworthy for being near a coastal highway and an air landing ground, and for having behind it an open plain suitable for maneuver. The final plan assigned 1st Infantry Division two Ranger Battalions and other supporting units as reserves, as well as six beaches on a total frontage of six miles. One regiment of the division was to move inland, link up with paratroopers near Niscemi, and move on the airfield at Ponte Olivo. The second regiment was to move toward the airfield also. The Ranger battalions were to take the town of Gela.

45th Infantry Division had before it a landing zone of fifteen miles in length. Immediately inland of the beach lay a broad plain. At a distance of about ten miles were situated the towns of Biscari and Comiso. These towns, and the airfields associated with them, constituted 45th Infantry Division's primary objective. One of the division's regiments was to land east of the mouth of the Acate River and drive north to capture Biscari and its airfield, as well as Ponte Dirillo, where the coastal highway crosses the Acate. A second regiment was responsible for taking Scoglitti and Vittoria. The division's final regiment had to seize the airfield at Comiso, while also maintaining contact with Eighth Army at Ragusa.

The portion of the 82d Airborne Division which would land before the primary invasion force was to lend support to the 1st Infantry Division by taking the ground near Gela to be in a position to defend against an enemy counterstroke from the north and east. These forces would come under the command of II Corps, and had been trained to occupy road intersections, not only to hold them open for American troops advancing from the beaches, but also to obstruct efforts by the enemy to move units to the beachhead in an effort to throw the invaders out.

The Allied plan called for the paratroops to be ferried aboard 227 C-47s under the command of the 52d Troop Carrier Wing. The aircraft were to drop their loads at the appointed zones between 11:30 PM July 9 and 12:06 AM July 10, and then return to their points of origination in North Africa. Because of fear of the naval convoys and their anti-aircraft arrays, the planners eschewed a short, straight flight over

Pantelleria in favor of a more circuitous route over Malta that required three sharp turns over water at night, and six hours flying time. In addition, no pathfinders were to go in ahead of the troop carriers, and hence the drop zones would not be marked. Pilots were required to commit distinguishing marks to memory and be able to discern them by moonlight. Finally, because of the enormity of the enterprise, and the demands which it placed upon Allied air forces, the paratroops were to receive no fighter protection, and would instead be forced to rely upon tactical surprise.

As might be anticipated, logistic considerations were paramount in an undertaking the size of the HUSKY operation. In the American zone of operations, 45th Infantry Division began with twenty-one days of maintenance and ten units of fire, all to be conveyed with the assault and in the first follow-up convoy on D plus 4. In the second follow-up convoy of D plus 8, this unit would receive seven more days maintenance and an additional one and one-sixth units of fire. Its partner in II Corps, 1st Infantry Division, went into action with seven days maintenance and two and one-third units of fire, and would receive from the D plus 4 follow up seven more days of maintenance and an additional one and one-sixth units of fire. The last follow up convoy, D plus 8, would bring this division fourteen more days maintenance and two and one-third units of fire. Third Infantry Division generally followed this plan except that it received about one half of the maintenance and fire units in the third follow up convoy.

In addition to the supplies specifically designated for each unit, the plan provided for sizable provisions to be placed aboard ships in North Africa and then transported to the landing zone for ready transfer ashore. Thus, almost three weeks worth of ammunition and supplies would be available from cargo vessels in the invasion area, beginning two weeks after the invasion. Yet further supplies, ammunition, weapons and equipment remained at Bizerte, ready for immediate shipment to Sicily.

A particularly noteworthy aspect of the HUSKY operation was the manner in which the Allies' logistics system had improved. This was observable primarily with regard to the Allies' amphibious equipment and its manner of use. Indeed, much new equipment was used in large numbers for the first time. The most prominent of these were four amphibious vehicles, namely the LCVP (landing craft, vehicle or personnel), the LST (landing ship, tank), the LCI (landing craft, infantry) and the LCT (landing craft, tank). All were intended to bring their cargoes to the water's edge and discharge them there

with speed and efficiency. Among Allied leaders, however, there was some anxiety about their performance for the simple reason that time had not permitted testing of the vehicles under all possible conditions. In contrast, another new piece of equipment, the DUKW (known, naturally enough, as "the duck"), enjoyed a high level of confidence. This amphibious truck was capable of 50 miles per hour on land and over 5 knots at sea, and had been designed to carry up to five thousand pounds of cargo, men and their equipment, and wounded. Seventh Army expected the DUKW alone to resolve many anticipated logistics problems.

The interrelationship among the respective army, navy and air force commands in anticipation of HUSKY was a curious one. One would expect that the services would be forced to confer regarding the matter of naval gunfire in support of the landing, and such conferences naturally took place. However, the two sides held opposite views from the outset on the question of whether naval gunfire should be used to "soften" the invasion beaches prior to the landings. The navy urged that such "softening fire" be used; the army argued, successfully as it turned out, that the fire should be withheld in the interest of achieving tactical surprise, and to protect paratroopers already on the ground. Both sides agreed that naval gunfire would be necessary and forthcoming in support of the infantry once it had come ashore.

While the navy and army were able to cooperate in establishing a fire support plan, the air force command steadfastly refused to work with either of them. There does not appear to be a compelling explanation for this behavior, and it is remarkable that Eisenhower tolerated it. In brief, the Allied air forces made it clear that they would not provide ground support until they had first succeeded in neutralizing the Axis air forces. Since the Allies lacked sufficient forces to perform both tasks at once, and since Allied air commanders were committed to the concept of massed forces, and finally since destruction of the Axis air forces was regarded as the primary objective, there would be no ground support until Allied air commanders were prepared to give it. As a result, the air plan issued in June failed to provide army and navy commanders with meaningful information as to what air support they could expect to have on the day of the invasion.

In spite of the shortcomings of the air plan, in fact quite sizable air support was made available for the Sicily invasion. The Northwest African Tactical Air Force (NATAF) provided twenty fighter squadrons on Malta, an American fighter group on Pantelleria, and yet another American fighter group on the isle of Gozo, near Malta. The aircraft thus amassed totaled almost 700. Added to these were additional fighter-bombers and tactical bombers operating from bases in North Africa. Some of these aircraft were designated to move to Sicily when captured airfields became available.

The Allied air forces which took part in HUSKY were organized under the umbrella of the Mediterranean Air Command (MAC), headed by Air Chief Marshal Sir Arthur Tedder, General Eisenhower's deputy commander for air operations in the invasion. MAC included Northwest African Air Forces (NAAF), the RAF, Middle East (RAFME) (which had the U.S. Ninth Air Force attached to it), and RAF Malta. NAAF, under the command of General Carl Spaatz, was made up principally of Northwest African Strategic Air Force (NASAF), Maj. Gen. James H. Doolittle commanding, and Northwest African Tactical Air Force (NATAF) under Air Vice Marshal Sir Arthur Coningham.[90] NASAF included four groups of American B-17s, five groups of American medium bombers (B-25s and B-26s) and four wings of RAF Wellingtons, as well as five American fighter groups, flying P-38s and P-40s. NATAF, whose purpose was almost entirely tactical in nature, included three additional groups of American medium bombers (A-20s and B-25s), two RAF and one South African wings of tactical bombers and two tactical reconnaissance squadrons.[91]

## HUSKY IN EXECUTION

### Pantelleria and Initial Landings

Eisenhower's first task in preparation for HUSKY was the reduction of the nearby island of Pantelleria, a small, volcanic island of forty-two square miles in area. It had been effectively closed to foreigners since 1926 while the Italians improved its defenses. It quartered a garrison of 10,000 men and possessed RDF stations and numerous airfields, so that it constituted a potential source of danger to the Allied force which would assault Sicily. Pantelleria had but one possible landing area, at the northwest end of the island near Porto di Pantelleria. As with most other Mediterranean islands, the terrain of Pantelleria is hilly, the highest point being found on Montagna Grande at 2,743 feet. The island's northern end included an airfield capable of handling four-engine bombers and a hangar 1100 feet long including an electric light plant, water supply and repair facilities. Pantelleria could accommodate more than eighty aircraft. Perhaps

more importantly, it had over one hundred gun emplacements.[92]

The fact that enemy aircraft could make use of the airfields on Pantelleria, if only for the purpose of monitoring the movements of Allied shipping, meant that maximum tactical surprise for HUSKY might well be in jeopardy. The island also housed a refueling station for Axis submarines. The capture of the island would not only deprive Axis forces of these advantages but also provide the Allies with additional airbases, and therefore the opportunity to cover Sicily in a way not otherwise possible. Having concluded that these purposes were worth securing, Eisenhower resolved to take the island. The method he selected was a massive air bombardment, a course of action that would avoid the problems which would confront landing attempts on the island's poor beaches. The Allies committed the entire NASAF to the operation, with the exception of the two wings of RAF Wellingtons. Since much of NATAF was to take part in the invasion, the Allies used only part of it for this operation. The result was that the Allied air forces numbered something less than 1000 aircraft, while their Axis opponents fielded a like number.[93]

The Allies commenced their air assault, and a complementary naval blockade, on May 18. By the end of May the Allies had succeeded in cutting the island off from any source of reinforcement or resupply. The air assault so disrupted the Axis forces and their infrastructure that after two weeks it was impossible for them to maintain any serviceable aircraft. Between June 6 and June 11 the Allies bombed the island virtually around the clock, culminating in a raid carried out by 1100 Allied aircraft. The enemy's ineffectual efforts to defend the island against the Allied onslaught did little more than cost him 60 aircraft. On June 8 the Royal Navy launched a full scale bombardment of Porto di Pantelleria.[94]

The Allies smothered the Axis gun positions on the island on the night of June 10/11. The landing craft began their assault at 10:30 AM on June 11, during which the Luftwaffe tried unsuccessfully to thwart the attack with large formations of fighter aircraft. The supporting naval forces began firing at shore targets thirty minutes later. Shortly thereafter the assault craft came ashore. The Axis forces surrendered six hours later. In the next few days the rest of the surrounding islands fell to the Allies.[95]

The air plan for HUSKY required that the main body of NAAF apply maximum force against the

---

90  Craven and Cate, v. II, p. 416.
91  Ibid., pp. 417-418.

92  Ibid., pp. 419-420.
93  Ibid., pp. 422-425.
94  Ibid., pp. 425-427.
95  Ibid., pp. 427-430.

Axis forces until D minus 7. At the same time, however, it was to support the build up for the invasion as well as interdict the enemy's lines of communication. Until the end of June the Allied air forces remorselessly bombed Axis airfields and the ports on Sicily. There were nineteen large airbases and a dozen newly developed fields on the island. The Allies attacked not only the bases around Catania, Gerbini, Comiso and Biscari, but also the bases in the western portion of the island. The Allied air forces also made attacks on Sardinia and Greece, and on enemy marshalling yards, supply depots, and ports along Italy's western coast.[96]

The Allies began heavy attacks on Messina and its corresponding ports across the straits on 18 June. More attacks followed throughout June and early July over Sicily, southern Italy and Sardinia. These were intended, in addition to their obvious military purposes, to confuse the enemy as to the Allies' ultimate intentions. The Axis forces responded without substantial effect. The Allies began the final phase of their pre-invasion air assault on July 2, for the purpose of eradicating any possible intervention by Axis air forces from Sicilian bases during the invasion. In addition, while Allied medium bombers subjected the airfields on eastern Sicily to intense bombardment, Allied strategic bombers assaulted southern Italy. As a result, by the eve of the invasion there were only two fully operational enemy airfields on Sicily. The Allies had eradicated the Axis airfields at Gerbini, and driven half of the enemy's Sicilian based aircraft to Italy. The Allied air assault cost the Axis forces about a thousand aircraft. As the invasion approached, the Allied air forces disposed of 4900 operational aircraft of all types, while their adversaries could counter with only about 1600 aircraft based not only on Sicily, but also in such relatively inconvenient places as Sardinia, Italy and southern France.[97]

As noted previously, the naval plan for *HUSKY* called for landings by British forces from the United Kingdom, the Middle East and Tunisia, and by American forces from both the United States and North Africa. Admiral Cunningham had designated Vice Admiral H. K. Hewitt as commander of the Western Naval Task Force. Rear Admirals A.G. Kirk, J. L Hall and R. L. Conolly commanded the U.S. landings in the *CENT, DIME* and *JOSS* sectors respectively. Admiral Cunningham designated Admiral Bertram Ramsay, the hero of Dunkirk, to command Eastern Naval Task Force. Ramsay nominated Rear Admiral Troubridge to command the British landings at *ACID NORTH, ACID SOUTH* and *BARK EAST*. For

the commander of the British assault at *BARK SOUTH*, Ramsay chose Rear Admiral R.R. McGrigor. He installed Rear Admiral Philip Vian as commander in the *BARK WEST* sector.[98] His selection to direct the activities of *FORCE H* was Vice Admiral A.U. Willis.

The invasion of Sicily began in North Africa with the embarkation of British and American paratroopers aboard transport aircraft and gliders, bound for delivery over Sicily during the night/early morning of July 9/10, 1943. Allied commanders had been somewhat apprehensive about this part of the *HUSKY* operation, because of their own lack of experience in directing paratroopers under combat conditions, and because the transport/glider stream would in part pass over the naval convoy, filled as it was with nervous anti-aircraft gunners anticipating the unfriendly arrival of Axis aircraft. The misgivings of Allied commanders turned out, in the event, to be well justified.

The plan for the Allied airborne assault on Sicily called for the simultaneous flight of more than 350 aircraft and more than 130 gliders to transport about 5000 paratroopers to Sicily, over an approach of 400 miles. On D-1, the British paratrooper contingent was to land in two zones near Syracuse, descending in 137 gliders between 10:10 PM and 10:30 PM. One force was to land in the western suburbs, while the other was to come down to the south of the city, its purpose to secure the canal bridge and railway, and prevent their demolition. Approximately one hour later, the 82nd Airborne Division was to drop from 220 C-47s at a point about four miles inland and six miles east of Gela, so as to control the beach exits in the landing area of the U.S. 1st Infantry Division. Both of these forces were required, according to the plan, to traverse somewhat circuitous routes in order to arrive at their drop zones.[99]

The conditions under which these airborne landings took place served to enhance their inherently dangerous qualities. The scant quarter moon was due to set shortly before midnight, thereby affording the landing force little in the way of visual support. Such little light as this moon did provide, and the navigational aids available to the aircrews, upon which they relied under conditions of radio silence, were eroded by weather conditions. During the afternoon and evening a strong wind had begun to blow, and by midnight it was blowing 40 miles per hour aloft. This

96  *Ibid.*, pp. 434-435.
97  *Ibid.*, pp. 437-445.
98  Roskill, v. III, p. 118.
99  General D.D. Eisenhower, "Dispatch on Sicilian Operations," 1943, p. 20, (hereinafter "Eisenhower Dispatch"), United States Marine Corps University Collection of World War II documents (hereinafter "USMC Collection."

caused both the British and American forces to become disoriented, some of both groups missing their first visual checkpoint at Malta. The aircraft began to straggle after one another in mixed formations, their approach being further inhibited by enemy flak. In addition, the preliminary air assault had resulted in fires and attendant smoke, obscuring final check points for the landing force.[100]

In the British sector these unfortunate circumstances led to even more unfortunate results. Many tow pilots released their charges prematurely, with the result that the British naval forces in the Eastern Task Force saw "the depressing sight of large numbers of gliders floating in the water" at 5 AM on D-day. About 47 gliders met their fate in this way; indeed, only 12 of the 137 gliders landed in the target zone, with the remaining 75 scattered in the southeastern part of the island. Similarly, the American parachutists were dispersed over a 60 mile pattern between Licata and Cap Noto.[101]

In spite of this rather dubious beginning, the Allied airborne troops performed well. A British force of only 8 officers and 65 men held the canal bridge south of Syracuse until 3:30 PM on D-day, and by that time only 4 officers and 15 men had not become casualties. They were just withdrawing when a relief force from the landing forces arrived to drive the enemy away from the bridge, which remained intact. The tiny force of paratroops stayed on to defend the bridge while the British 17th Infantry Brigade, 5th Division, advanced across it. Contemporaneously, the American paratroops held the high ground in the Gela area to prevent enemy reinforcements from reaching the beach, an action credited with speeding the subsequent advance from the beachhead by 48 hours.[102]

Even the widely dispersed paratroop forces gave a good account of themselves. The British 1st Airlanding Brigade, which landed in the southeast, attacked the Italian posts vigorously, thereby disorganizing the beach defenses and reserves. Elements of the U.S. 505th Parachute Regimental Combat Team achieved decisive results. Its 3rd Battalion seized the high ground near Vittoria and held it against German tanks until relieved by the landing forces. The 2nd Battalion captured the town of Marina di Ragusa, making contact with the U.S. 45th Infantry Division on D+1. As a result of these aggressive activities, the 505th RCT captured 20-30,000 Italian prisoners.[103]

Attached to the 505th RCT as naval gunfire liai-

son officers were Ensigns G. A. Hulten and R. M. Seibert, both of whom were qualified parachutists and had volunteered for duty with the 505th RCT. They had both received three weeks training with their assigned unit before the invasion. Enemy gunfire killed Hulten shortly after the paratroops touched down; Seibert survived to report his experience.

Hulten and Seibert were the only naval liaison officers attached to the entire Regimental Combat Team, even though pre-invasion intelligence had shown that tanks and reserve troop concentrations could be expected in the landing area. To make up for this obvious shortcoming, "the Regiment agreed to supply material and assistance as required." The shortage of Navy personnel, however, was not the only difficulty to be overcome. The Regimental Combat Team had failed to assign to the naval officers a separate radio or crew for communicating with the ships lying offshore. In fact, the liaison officers could only perform their tasks indirectly, since all radio transmissions had to be made on the 505th RCT's network. Hulton and Seibert could only reach their base ship, the USS Boise, through the 7th Field Artillery Regiment. Finally, although it had originally been intended that the two ensigns should act as a team for spotting and directing fire, on the eve of the invasion the Regimental Combat Team assigned one officer to the First Battalion and the other to the Third Battalion, thereby reducing their effectiveness.[104]

The task of the 505th Regimental Combat Team was to land at a road junction near Niscemi and secure both the road and the surrounding high ground in order to forestall movement of enemy troops toward the beach. It was also to seize and mine nearby bridges and assert control over local secondary roads and a neighboring rail line. In the event, what befell the 505th RCT was typical of the fate shared by many of its sister units. The pilots missed their navigational landmarks, and after circling once in an effort to locate the correct drop zone, disgorged the paratroopers along a 25 mile strip in a southeasterly direction, almost to San Croce de Camerina. One of the aircraft near Seibert was shot down, thereby fully illuminating the landing area, so that enemy troops arrived on the scene in very short order. The paratroopers were naturally quite disorganized by these events, and there was continuous sharp skirmishing throughout the night as the Americans tried to collect themselves

---

[100]   *Ibid.*, p. 21.
[101]   *Ibid.*
[102]   *Ibid.*
[103]   *Ibid.*

[104]   Memorandum from Ensign Robert M. Seibert, D-V(G) USNR to Force Gunnery Officer; Subject: Operation HUSKY, 21 July 1943, p. 1, USMC Collection, Box 117, File No. 23.

and in the process came in contact with Axis patrols. Another consequence of the miscarried drop, in addition to the presence of thoroughly alerted enemy troops, was that the paratroopers were unable to remove all of the equipment bundles to the Combat Team Command Post. As a result, the Regimental Combat Team did not establish communications on schedule. [105]

Following these initial engagements, the enemy counterattacked in earnest with tanks and supporting infantry, "threatening to annihilate our own infantry and to break through to the beach." The 505th RCT managed to retrieve the situation, however, by making contact with the Shore Fire Control Party attached to the 45th Infantry Division, which was operating in the same general area. By this means Seibert's unit was able to direct naval fire against the tanks and disrupt the enemy's infantry assault. It was necessary, however, for suitable anti-tank guns to be brought forward before the attack could be turned back and the lost ground recovered. [106]

These initial airborne landings, while suffering from the effects of the weather, nevertheless enjoyed a considerable measure of success. Subsequent airborne operations, in particular that of the 504th RCT on the night of D+1 in the area of Gela, did not fare as well. This flight, which had been postponed one day from its original scheduled launch, suffered immediately from the fact that the invasion fleet rimming the southeastern shore of the island received insufficient warning of its approach. In addition, the flight course now followed the actual battle front for 35 miles, and the Allied antiaircraft gunners on both land and sea had now become accustomed by two days of air attack to shoot on sight. Added to this was the unfortunate circumstance that the air transports approached the ships shortly after an enemy air raid. In the resulting "friendly fire," 23 transports were shot down, and the half of the remaining aircraft so badly damaged that they eventually had to be scrapped. These unfortunate circumstances were compounded by a wide dispersal of the parachutists from Gela to the east coast, resulting from faulty navigation. The unscheduled arrival of these troops in the Allied zone of operations led to fatal confusion. The 1st Infantry Division G-2 report carried the 504th RCT as an unidentified German parachute regiment. In a move to the Allied rear area, the 504th RCT suffered casualties in excess of many units in combat. Twenty to twenty-five percent of the 5000 American parachutists involved became casualties. Admiral Hewitt laid the responsibility for this inci-

dent at the feet of the air force. According to Hewitt, while the air force had informed the navy of the inbound and outbound routes for the transports "by dispatch to the forces at sea," the navy never received these plans in writing. Indeed, air force planners had not submitted the issue of transport routing in the assault zone to the navy and army commanders, so that the latter could consider the implications of the plan. Hewitt's view was that the route ultimately selected was unsuitable to the navy. Even more egregious, however, was the fact that "this unilateral decision" about transport routes was unassailable by the naval commander, since he became aware of it only after the imposition of radio silence. In consequence, according to Hewitt, the paratroop transports arrived over the naval transports from the same direction as the enemy "simultaneously with enemy dive bombers." [107]

A later British airborne operation encountered similar problems. For reasons not known, the routing of this mission was delayed, and so therefore was notification of it to the convoys along the route. The force consisted of 2,000 men in 31 gliders and 105 troop carriers. Twenty-six of the aircraft returned early because of engine trouble or the intense flak over the drop zone. What now ensued over the Allied fleet was not pretty. A "most confusing air defense situation" was reported between 9:30 PM and midnight by the Senior Officer of the HMS *Wishart*, in escort of a follow-up convoy near Syracuse. This was due to the fact that while news of the approach of friendly aircraft had been communicated to the escort force during the afternoon of D+3, it had not been relayed to all of the ships by dark. This situation was complicated by the presence of enemy aircraft in the area at the same time. In consequence, the merchant ships opened fire on the transports as they flew directly overhead. Allied antiaircraft fire accounted for eleven airplanes, and damaged a considerable number more. [108]

In spite of these tribulations, the British force successfully prosecuted its mission, which was to seize and hold a bridge over the Simeto river, thus securing for the landing troops the only exit from the high ground into the plain of Catania. The airborne force was able to marshal 200 troopers with 5 anti-tank guns, and these were able to capture the bridge and remove its demolition charges. While eventually these men were forced to retire, the bridge was shortly recaptured by elements of the XIII Corps, still in its intact condition. [109]

---

[105] *Ibid.*
[106] *Ibid.*, pp. 1-2;

[107] Eisenhower Dispatch, p. 22.
[108] *Ibid.*, p. 23.
[109] Eisenhower Dispatch, p. 23.

While both Patton and Montgomery later testified to the significance of these airborne operations to the overall success of the entire enterprise, those successes had been achieved at substantial cost. In order to decrease the chances that such a sequence of events would not in future be repeated, Eisenhower appointed a board of review concerning the matter on July 23.[110]

In anticipation of the invasion, Admiral Cunningham moved to Malta on July 4, and Eisenhower and Alexander followed him there on July 7. According to Eisenhower, his chief anxieties were the weather and enemy reconnaissance. He reported that he and his staff had expected to have lost surprise by the morning of D-1, it having been assumed that, notwithstanding the successes of the Allied air strikes, the enemy should have acquired knowledge of the invasion fleet through their reconnaissance aircraft. On that day, moreover, it was known that two German aircraft had seen part or all of the invasion fleet. The Supreme Commander also received reports that the German forces on the island were moving purposefully about, apparently having raised the alarm on at least the western half of Sicily. Nevertheless, by the time the assault actually went in, the command staff was convinced that both tactical and strategic surprise had been achieved, as evidenced by the fact that the enemy troops defending the beach areas quite obviously had received little if any warning of the armada's approach. The weather, as it turned out, was the area about which the Supreme Commander could rightly have been concerned. A strong northwest wind began to blow on the night of D-1, and its effect on the airborne operations has already been noted. The wind blew at thirty-five miles an hour in the zone of the Western Naval Task Force, and while this posed obvious and continuous problems for the landing force, it also had a deleterious effect on those enemy forces defending the beaches.[111]

While the weather conditions caused delays in the arrival of some of the landing craft, notably in the area of the 45th Infantry Division, where the assault was delayed by an hour, nonetheless the supporting naval gunfire was devastating to the enemy. Likewise, Allied aircraft pounded the enemy from Gozo, Malta and Pantelleria, and on D-Day 1200 fighter sorties were flown. Both heavy and medium Allied bombers continued to strike Axis airfields and communications. The Allied air effort was aided by the early capture of enemy airbases at Pachino and Gela on D-Day, Comiso on the night of D+1, and Ponte Olivo and Biscari on D+2. An RAF fighter wing relocated to Pachino on D+3.[112]

Eisenhower went ashore at Licata on July 12 after having visited Admiral Hewitt aboard the *USS Monrovia*. "There was hardly a shell or a bomb to be heard, and the outstanding impression was one of complete serenity. Landing craft were proceeding on their lawful occasions from ship to shore; it looked more like a huge regatta than an operation of war." Thus convinced of the successful launch of the invasion, Eisenhower returned to Tunis via Malta.[113]

Eisenhower later observed that "[T]he landings in general did not encounter serious opposition. Shore batteries did not put up vigorous resistance; some were not even manned at the time of attack; those which caused trouble were for the most part quickly silenced; there was sporadic rifle and machine gun fire." The British in particular enjoyed favorable conditions. The 5th Division and 50th Division encountered only light resistance; the 231st Brigade got ashore and inland very quickly, and the 51st Division "had no particular difficulty." Canadian 1st Division "got ashore against indifferent opposition and were able to press quickly inland." A British Commando force made "a perfectly coordinated assault on one of the coastal batteries, only to discover that the guns were dummies."[114]

So weak had been the Italian opposition, in fact, that Admiral Ramsay cautioned that "the success of the assaults in HUSKY cannot be considered as a reliable guide to what may be attempted or achieved elsewhere."

> The assaults in HUSKY were uniformly successful due to the low state of preparedness of some of the coast defenders and the lack of resolution showed by those who were alert. They are thus only of limited value for the deduction of lessons for the future. It is believed that the poor showing of the Italians on the day was largely due to their being overwhelmed by the weight of our initial assaults, delivered as they were with a considerable degree of local tactical surprise.[115]

Admiral Ramsay observed that casualties to shipping and amongst landing craft were considerably less

---

[110]   *Ibid.*

[111]   *Ibid.*, p.24.

[112]   *Ibid.*, p. 25.

[113]   *Ibid.*

[114]   *Ibid.*

[115]   Vice Admiral Bertram H. Ramsay, RN, "Operation 'HUSKY.' Report of Naval Commander Eastern Task Force," October, 1943, p. 1, (hereinafter "Ramsay Report") USMC Collection; Ibid, Appendix V, p.1.

than had been anticipated and allowed for. He considered this to be due to: (a) the very high degree of air superiority achieved, (b) the efficiency of the anti-submarine organization, and (c) the unexpected attainment of a considerable degree of tactical surprise. Ramsay concluded that tactical surprise had resulted from a combination of circumstances, namely the adoption of a waxing moon period for the assaults, the lack of enemy air reconnaissance on D-1 day and a prolonged period of "alert" preceding D Day, and the unexpected high wind that arose on the afternoon of D-1. These factors, Ramsay believed, had lulled the enemy coast defenses into a false sense of security. [116]

## The Naval Experience

The Allies spent the period between June 22 and July 4, 1943 carrying out rehearsals of the assault landing and in special training of task groups. The time was also used to install special equipment. Because of the proximity of enemy aircraft and submarines, these rehearsals were not full scale. Nevertheless, the Allies managed to conduct three complete naval rehearsals and one combined rehearsal. Unfortunately, these were not always carried out with the same craft, as other commitments, mechanical breakdowns and re-fittings took some boats out of service. Even so, by the time HUSKY was commenced in earnest, all craft had performed their roles at least once, and some had done so several times. In addition, all brigades conducted individual combined rehearsals, and many combined signal exercises were carried out. [117]

Admiral Hewitt commanded over six hundred ships and landing craft, one hundred and thirty of which were allocated for escort, covering and fire support. On July 9 the weather was unfavorable for convoys, with the wind velocity at about 35 knots and a moderate sea. The LSTs had difficulty making 8 knots, and the LCIs and smaller craft were making heavy weather of it. The LCT convoy proceeded independently and there was considerable doubt whether the LCT tank waves would arrive at the assault beaches in time to support the infantry. The JOSS Force LSTs and LCIs, in spite of the wind and sea conditions, pushed on as hard as they could in order to meet H-hour. This resulted in some LSTs lagging behind to the extent that they lost sight of the next group ahead, so that some craft became separated from their proper groups and anchored in the wrong area of the beachhead. The Control Ships, acting as escorts during the approach, likewise became separated and were not in their proper positions in

the rendezvous areas to assemble and lead the assault LCVPs to the beach. [118]

Three British submarines acted as beacons, taking up positions in the Gulf of Gela on July 7. On July 8, low flying aircraft caused *Seraph* and *Shakespeare* to dive; that evening, an E-Boat forced down *Seraph*. These submarines left for Malta on D- day; a Ju 88 attacked *Safari* without success; *Seraph* rescued a U.S. soldier fallen overboard. [119]

Opposition was light on all beaches with the exception of YELLOW, RED 2 and GREEN 2. The surf was about three feet high, and many landing craft broached. In the CENT area, delays in loading boats prompted the attack force commander to order postponement of H-Hour to 3:45 AM. Landings were generally unopposed, due to the pre-assault cruiser and destroyer shore bombardment. The 157th Regimental Combat Team landed on its assigned beaches, moved inland and captured the designated initial objectives ahead of schedule. The 179th Regimental Combat Team landed on the correct beaches, but experienced delay in movement through the dunes because of extensive mine fields. The 180th Regimental Combat Team gained its assigned D-day objectives after completing a successful landing. However, the landing was not on the correct beaches, and this caused delay in marching and forming up. [120]

In the JOSS area initial attack waves landed according plan in spite of delay caused by bad weather. The landings were over the correct beaches according to schedule in spite of some enemy fire. There was not much fire on GREEN, YELLOW and BLUE beaches; however, there was considerable artillery and machinegun fire on RED beach. [121]

In Admiral Ramsay's operational area, the LCT convoy for BARK EAST had been held up by the weather and had eventually made BARK SOUTH, arriving nearly six hours late. Similar convoys for ACID and for BARK SOUTH were each about two hours late. The most timely was the LCT convoy for BARK WEST, which arrived only thirty minutes late. [122]

The ships at the release positions in the British naval sector were apparently not detected by the shore defenses, and the only difficulties experienced in lowering and forming up landing craft were those imposed by the weather. The defenses were taken

[116]  Ramsay Report, p. 1.
[117]  *Ibid.*, Appendix V, p. 2.

[118]  Commander Western Naval Task Force (Vice Admiral H. K. Hewitt), "Action Report: The Sicilian Campaign, Operation HUSKY, July-August, 1943, p. 37 (hereinafter "Hewitt report"), USMC Collection.
[119]  *Ibid.*
[120]  *Ibid.*, p. 38.
[121]  *Ibid.*, p. 40.
[122]  Ramsay Report, p. 4.

generally by surprise when the assaulting formations landed and there was little organized resistance on the beaches. A proportion of the coast defenses were not, in fact, manned on that night; those that were manned were, in the majority of cases, not stoutly fought. At first light there was a certain amount of shelling from shore batteries, but these were effectively dealt with by supporting monitors, destroyers and gun boats. The effectiveness of the supporting fire from British naval forces was remarked upon by friend and foe alike. [123]

Because of the late arrival of the LCT convoys the only LCTs to beach before daylight were those at BARK SOUTH. The unloading of the ships was commenced without delay, and proceeded satisfactorily, despite bad exits and soft sand in the ACID sector and false beaches and soft sand at BARK WEST. Both the LST and the LCI proved, in Admiral Ramsay's view, invaluable in their respective roles, and he considered that the speed with which both vehicles and personnel were landed was one of the principal factors in the success of the operation from the naval point of view. Although at times the rate at which stores were unloaded appeared to be disappointing, the totals unloaded for the beaches were, in fact, greater than the planned figures. [124]

Neither BARK SOUTH nor BARK EAST were worked to capacity during HUSKY. The LST, LCI and the DUKW fulfilled the highest expectations of the British. They considered that the beach organizations worked satisfactorily, and that the shortage of transport ashore to clear the beach dumps resulted from the very quick forward advance of the army. Admiral Ramsay observed, however, that "[T]his is not likely ... to obtain in future operations undertaken against a more determined enemy." [125]

The general absence of enemy air attacks in Admiral Ramsay's sector was as surprising in its extent and considerably greater than the British had been led to expect. According to the Admiral, British ships were not attacked until 10:15 AM on July 10 when the enemy raided the ships at ACID beach. On subsequent days there were intermittent air attacks, principally on the East coast, and an increasing number occurred at night. Ramsay considered it fortunate that more damage was not done by these attacks; only three transport ships and a hospital ship were sunk as a result of them. The enemy attacked and sank the hospital ship *Talamba* and also attacked the *ABA* and *Dorsetshire*, all of which were assailed while lying over five miles from land and fully illuminated. Ram-

say had ordered that all such hospital ships remain darkened and with the fleet at night and that full illumination would only be switched on when the ships were five miles clear of the beaches and on passage to or from the assault area. After the sinking of the *Talamba* the British kept all hospital ships with the fleet all night without lights. [126]

In the CENT area, destroyers were used to cover and support the landing. They opened preparatory fire at fifteen minutes before H-hour; each destroyer was assigned an area of responsibility and covered it with 5 inch shells. As a result, 45th Infantry Division landed practically unopposed. [127] Stores, ammunition and supplies were distributed along several miles of beaches. Exits were few, difficult and mined. Several boats were lost on the rocks of GREEN 2 and YELLOW 2 beaches and casualties were sustained. In the DIME area, the beaches were heavily mined and bulldozers, DUKWs and other vehicles were lost. In the JOSS area, the GREEN beaches proved to be the most hazardous; the entrance was rocky, and the shallowness of the beach made it impossible to retract or to render assistance to those beached until succeeding waves landed. Most boats were stuck on the sand. LSTs had great difficulty because of soft sand on RED beach; so they were unloaded at either YELLOW or BLUE beaches or in Licata harbor [128]

The original attack plan had called for the softening of the beach defenses by paratroops, whose intervention was deemed vital to the success of the seaborne assaults, so that the dropping of the paratroops effectively determined D-day and H-Hour (July 10, 2:45 AM, or two hours before first light). To Admiral Hewitt's great regret, the plan was later changed, so that the role of the paratroops became not the softening of the beaches, but the seizure of high ground round Gela and the capture of the airfield at Ponte Olivo; the date and time of the invasion, however, remained the same, even though Hewitt regarded both as "unsuitable from a naval viewpoint." [129]

The Appreciation of FORCE 141, which originally called out the role of the paratroops, stated that the selected date would "afford the approach to the coastline the cover of darkness." The fact was, however, that the assault forces were required to make the approach to the beaches in a brilliant waxing moon which would not set until the vessels had hove to in the initial transport areas immediately under the coast defense guns of the enemy. These facts were well known to the naval planners, who pointed out

[123]    *Ibid.*
[124]    *Ibid.*, p. 5.
[125]    *Ibid.*

[126]    *Ibid.;* Appendix V, pp. 9, 11.
[127]    Hewitt Report, p. 41.
[128]    *Ibid.*
[129]    *Ibid.*, p. 43.

the fact that the moon phase selected was most unfavorable for naval purposes. The date for the landing, however, was not changed because it was reiterated that this phase of the moon was most favorable to the dropping of the paratroops who were the only means available to "neutralize the beach defenses opposing the seaborne assaults." The time for the landing (2:45 AM) had been fixed by the fact that it required the paratroops about three hours from dropping time to assemble and carry out their mission of the "softening of the beaches"; in fact, however, ultimately the paratroops were directed away from the beach defenses. [130]

Since the softening of the beach defenses was vital to the whole plan, naval planners then suggested the employment of naval gunfire against beach defenses. This was not acceptable to the Army on the ground that "surprise" (a "fundamental principle of war") was to be achieved in the assault. Since H-hour required the Allied transports to be in the initial transport areas in brilliant moonlight, the prospect was remote that the enemy would fail to observe such a concentration of hostile shipping off his shores. It was apparent, moreover, that any illumination of the Allied forces, either accidentally by the Allies or purposefully by the enemy, would alert the enemy and disclose Allied intentions. Further, since heavy Allied pre-invasion bombing and the dropping of paratroops had preceded H-hour by almost three hours, the idea that surprise could be preserved was illusory. It was the naval viewpoint that surprise on the assault beaches was not feasible, and indeed not necessary provided there was a rapid seizure of a beachhead.

Owing to the limited capacity of the LCVPs, many trips to and from the beach were required to move any great quantity of supplies, creating operational fatigue in boat crews. The LCVP was a reliable and rugged boat but easily swamped upon beaching unless promptly unloaded. Many boats were ordered away from congested beaches and returned to their ships without unloading. DUKWs were loaded in LSTs and LCTs for the initial purpose of assisting in the unloading of the combat loaders. The problem was that after the first trip to shore, few of these vehicles returned to the ships for further loading, having been diverted by the army for employment onshore. This diversion of the DUKWs not only interrupted the unloading plan, but led to the loss of many DUKWs.

The adoption of the so-called "Montgomery Plan" had serious implications for the Western Naval Task Force. Not only were the beaches required for the Plan inferior for the assault, but also the problem of maintenance reached serious proportions. The beaches south of the Gela River, and particularly those south of the Acate River, introduced unusual natural obstacles. These beaches were backed by soft sand dunes, with undulations reaching a height of from 40 to 80 feet, for a distance of one-half mile to one mile from the sea. Barren slopes and patches of thick shrub bordered the landward side of these vast dunes. Cart tracks running parallel to the beaches lay between the shore line and the nearest metalled road located from one to three miles from the sea. Exits from the beaches to the hinterland were non-existent. The fact that many beaches were flanked by groups of rocks, and all beaches were bordered to seaward by bars or runnels, indicated that there would be difficulties in beaching landing craft, and in preventing stranding unless unloading of the boats was accomplished with special dispatch. The locale and condition of the landing beaches thus suggested the need for reinforced Shore Parties, with particular emphasis on road construction units to prepare exits from the beaches; increased motor vehicle transportation to move stores from beaches to inland dumps and to the advancing troops; and finally a greatly increased labor force to quickly unload boats and craft at the beaches. [131]

In the event, the organization and operation of the beaches during the assault phase presented some of the greatest difficulties in the HUSKY operation. The recurring delay in getting boats unloaded after the first few hours of the assault was present on all the CENT and DIME beaches, and to a lesser extent on the JOSS beaches. From about noon on D-day to the night of D+1, after the assault troops had reached inland objectives and were well engaged with the enemy, demands for ammunition and equipment were greatest. At the same time, the invasion force was inferior to the enemy in artillery and possibly in infantry. It was at this critical period that boat crews and shore parties fell behind in unloading, when the beaches became congested, and when there was a grave danger of complete breakdown in the supply system. [132]

Admiral Hewitt found the Beach Battalions to be the weakest link in the naval organization, while at the same time faced with one of the most arduous and difficult tasks.

During the assault phase of the operation the efficiency of the beach parties was no better than that of the shore parties of which they

[130] *Ibid.*

[131] *Ibid.*, p. 54.
[132] *Ibid.*, p. 57.

were a part. As the engineers of the shore parties became primarily involved in normal combat missions, with little concern for the operation of the beaches, the beach parties failed similarly in the prompt and full execution of their responsibilities. There was no concerted effort made to carry out prompt hydrographic surveys at first light on D day. Since thorough surveys were not promptly carried out by all the beach parties, there was a dearth of channel markers. This resulted in LCTs and LSTs standing in to beaches to unload without any guidance as to favorable or unfavorable sites, resulting in the grounding of some craft some distance from shore and causing delays in beaching. In view of the dependence upon the successful employment of pontoon causeways, the off-shore investigations should have been planned in detail and executed promptly with the break of dawn. Since the beach party is not provided a boat from which to carry out this off-shore work, beachmasters have had to confiscate boats to do this work. [133]

Hewitt pointed out that while so-called traffic control boats were supposed to accompany supply boats following the assault craft to the beaches, the traffic control boats failed to materialize, leaving the supply boats to land without direction. As a result, congestion on the beaches followed, a condition aggravated by the fact that the loads remained unloaded, owing to the failure of the Shore Party to perform this part of its task. In consequence, literally dozens of fully loaded supply craft were swamped or stranded ashore, so that the beaches were unavailable to following craft. Many supply craft sat unloaded for as long as 20 hours. [134]

Hewitt complained that there was a general lack of communication between the Shore Party and vessels such as LSTs moving in to land. This was in part due to the wide dispersal of Shore Party personnel over the beaches, where "[D]iscipline, leadership, and control were absent." Changes were made to the CENT beaches as many as eight times during the first two days of the assault, on the ground that beaches with better exits were being sought. This particularly irked Hewitt, who pointed out that the absence of suitable exits had been "conclusively shown" during the preliminary planning stages for the invasion. The planners had recommended that exits and roads would have to be constructed by the Shore Party, and

Hewitt claimed to have personally recommended that the CENT area have available an enhanced corps of road construction troops so that the problem could be resolved on D-day. [135]

Hewitt had under his command three navy Beach Battalions, one assigned to each of the CENT, JOSS and DIME force beach areas. He complained that because of the unsatisfactory conditions on these beaches, including the fact that the Beach Battalions lacked the proper equipment, the members of these units were engaged in pursuits not related to their main task, including loading and unloading boats, trucks and ships, road building, serving as gun crews, and acting as guards for POWs. The Beach Battalions stayed on their beaches for periods of weeks performing tasks for which they were not trained or equipped. Many of these troops were incapacitated by fever, malaria and dysentery. Hewitt accordingly believed that in addition to being more lavishly equipped, these units should be better trained. In particular, he believed that they required "more navy life," meaning that they should receive intensive shipboard training in order to instill in them "the necessary naval background." They should be taught

clean and orderly living in the field, how to get along with little and make that little do, how to take care of arms, equipment, and clothing and the necessity for doing so. Physical fitness, military courtesy and discipline should be emphasized in this training which should include overhead firing and other battle courses. These units are seamen first, and they should be garbed in a distinctive uniform in order that they may be distinguished on the beach. Helmets should be painted and marked so as to identify them as members of the Beach Party. [136]

Hewitt was convinced that many of the problems on the beaches could be traced to command issues.

Many of the failings... have been due to the lack of rank, experience, and personality of the Beachmasters. Such officers become submerged in numbers and seniority of the Army ashore. They lack the necessary rank and assurance to stand up against the constant succession of conflicting requests, orders, instructions and commands received on the spot from higher ranking Army officers, who are interested in getting one particular task

---

[133]   *Ibid.*, p. 58.
[134]   *Ibid.*

[135]   *Ibid.*, p. 59.
[136]   *Ibid.*, p. 61.

done, but have no immediate interest in the overall beach task. Many high ranking Army officers, not in the Shore Party, call upon the Beachmaster to subordinate his tasks in the behalf of this seniors' peculiar interests, notwithstanding the capabilities and limitations of the Beach Party. Naval officers of suitable rank, experience, and quality can cope with such interferences and prevent diversion of effort.

The sole exception to this pattern was on the JOSS beaches, where Group Commanders, all Captains and Commanders, "were very effective in bringing the JOSS beaches from disorder to efficiency." [137]

Similar complaints, in reference to the beaches in the British area of operations, were made by Admiral Ramsay. He found that "[B]each parties were not as well trained in the full scope of their duties as they should have been, and this fact was adversely remarked on by senior army officers." According to Ramsay, however, this deficiency was corrected by the time the operation took place, so that "in general it may be said that the naval beach parties carried out their duties very creditably." In spite of this success, however, Ramsay echoed his American counterpart, recommending that in future beach parties be commanded by Lieutenant Commanders, with senior Lieutenants "of character" to assist them. Observing that the officers attached to the beach party on BARK SOUTH were "very keen and hard working," he nevertheless concluded that they "had not the personality, experience or seniority to take complete charge of these beaches." The ability to take control of such a situation, especially in the dark or adverse weather conditions, would be crucial to success in any future similar operation. [138]

Operating in the Scoglitti area during the first four days of the operation was Destroyer Squadron 15, commanded by one C.C. Hartman aboard his flagship, the USS *Mervine*. In addition to this vessel, the squadron included eight other destroyers, all of them mounting 5 inch guns, as well as both 40mm and 20mm cannon. Prior to the assault, seven of the squadron's ships acted as a screen for the transport groups, while the remaining two ships were on detached duty, escorting LSTs from Tunis to the Scoglitti area. During the invasion, three of the squadron's vessels served in a screening role with vessels from another squadron, while the remainder of Destroyer Squadron 15 provided fire support. Until July 13 the squadron's vessels continued to alternate

between screen duty and fire support. [139]

Late on the evening of July 9, as the squadron lay off shore at Scoglitti, the weather was highly favorable for the invasion, as indeed it would be for several days thereafter. Between 10:20 PM and 11:35 PM, Hartman's squadron stood on station, prepared for the beginning of the assault. During that time, the crews observed steadily increasing activity on the island, including repeated incidents of heavy anti-aircraft fire, flare detonations, and even searchlights. Hartman believed that most of this activity was directed at Allied bombers and transport aircraft carrying Allied paratroopers. Indeed, one flight of American bombers flew over the squadron at a height of less than 600 feet heading south, giving Hartman and his crews "quite a start." Fortunately for the airmen, they had the presence of mind to switch on their running lights, so that the ships held their fire. [140]

At about 3:00 AM on July 10, after nearly an hour's delay, the assault vessels began moving in. Between 3:45 AM and 4:20 AM Destroyer Squadron 15 poured supporting fire on the beach area, against non-existent opposition. The assault waves were then safely ashore. Shortly thereafter, as small force of enemy bombers attacked the transport ships, although apparently without much effect. Hartman's ships continued to provide fire support, silencing even small caliber guns or batteries. In fact, the firing of the squadron's own guns was perhaps the most excitement experienced by the crews in the invasion. Neither the ships nor the troops landing met with resistance from the enemy ashore, and the enemy's naval forces made no appearance from the seaward side to harass Hartman's men. So complete was victory for Destroyer Squadron 15 in the Sicily invasion that it suffered no casualties whatever. [141]

The USS *Monrovia*, commanded by T. B. Brittain, had what for her crew must have been a particularly interesting experience during the first few days of the HUSKY operation. Although the *Monrovia* acted as a transport vessel, it embarked with "the Naval Commander Western Task Force, his operational staff, Fighter Control Group, the Commanding General Seventh Army, his Deputy Commander, full staff and a large Headquarters Detachment of various units. All together 126 officers, 670 men." The ship also carried many tons of equipment, fuel and

[137] *Ibid.*

[138] Ramsay Report, Appendix IV, p. 1; Ramsay Report, p. 15.

[139] Memorandum from C.C. Hartman, Commander Destroyer Squadron Fifteen to Commander-in-Chief, U.S. Fleet; Subject: Action Report—Assault on Scaglotti, Sicily and adjacent Area, July 9-13, 1943, pp. 1-2, USMC Collection, Box 117, File No. 27.

[140] *Ibid.*, p. 3; Enclosure A, p. 1 (Friday, 9 July).

[141] *Ibid.*, Enclosure A, p. 2 (Saturday, 10 July).

ammunition. The combination of so many dignitaries and so much cargo meant that the *Monrovia* was unable to directly participate in the assault. Instead, it furnished boats, boat crews and boat officers to two other vessels to assist them in getting the assault waves ashore. These conditions also extended unloading operations over a period of three days, when under normal circumstances the unloading would have taken half that time. [142]

The progress of the invasion in the sector of DIME Force on July 10 may be glimpsed from the *Monrovia*'s activities on that day. At shortly after midnight on July 10, *Monrovia* moved into the transport area to which it had been assigned and began to lower boats. At 8:43 AM it anchored off the island, and by 9:00 AM it began to discharge cargo, and continued to do so for the rest of that day. The next day, the *Monrovia* continued to unload cargo, and in the midmorning Admiral Hewitt debarked with some staff officers for an inspection tour. During this day, however, *Monrovia* was attacked by enemy aircraft on three separate occasions, suffering some minor damage. In one such attack, aircraft damaged and sank a merchant ship anchored quite near the *Monrovia*. [143]

July 12 was a particularly noteworthy date for the crew of the *Monrovia*. At 6:30 AM that morning, General Eisenhower came aboard for a conference with Admiral Hewitt and General Patton. The Supreme Commander and his staff stayed aboard for approximately one hour and twenty minutes, shortly after which *Monrovia* completed unloading its cargo. Shortly before noon, however, Vice Admiral Lord Louis Mountbatten and his party came aboard and stayed for two hours. At approximately 5:00 PM General Patton and his staff and equipment disembarked, and an hour later the *Monrovia* joined a convoy and its destroyer escort to leave the area. [144]

At least as far as the *Monrovia* was concerned, the resistance offered by the enemy in the *DIME* force sector appears to have been minimal. For example, in discussing the conduct of his officers and men, Brittain noted that "[T]hey made their landings and disembarked their troops in the face of such opposition as was present on the assigned beaches." Only two members of the ship's crew were wounded, neither of them seriously, and the crew expended relatively little ammunition. The only damage suffered by the *Monrovia* was to its engine room, sustained when a bomb from a Heinkel 111 exploded in the water on the ship's port side. This damage was minor, and the crew quickly repaired it. [145]

Brittain recommended one of his crew, seaman second class Thomas B. McMonagle, for the Navy Cross in connection with his actions during the assault. The story of this seaman's bravery is an interesting one. However, it also illustrates the relatively light enemy resistance encountered in the DIME sector. McMonagle was the coxswain in command of *Monrovia*'s Boat 31. He landed his boat at the appointed beach, during which operation he was wounded by enemy machine gun fire. Most interestingly, his commanding officer then reports that "[T]he Army boat team refused to embark even though the ramp was down and the boat well beached." In view of this, McMonagle backed the boat off the beach, silenced the enemy machine guns with his boat's weapons, and then re-landed the boat farther down the beach. The seaman continued to maintain control of the boat and returned her to the ship to which he had been assigned, all the while refusing to be relieved by his crew. Only when he was overcome by weakness would he relinquish control of the boat. [146]

The story of seaman McMonagle further shows that the Axis troops did not offer a blistering defense in the DIME area of operations. McMonagle, after all, was able to beach his boat twice, encountering only enemy machine gun fire, and silencing even that with his own weapons, and apparently without assistance in the form of naval gunfire or air support. It seems unlikely that McMonagle and his men were successful in killing all of the enemy machine gunners from the deck of a moving assault craft; the more plausible explanation is that they abandoned their posts after having first offered token resistance. The most interesting aspect of the McMonagle saga, however, would seem to be the refusal of the Army boat team to leave Boat 31 in the face of enemy resistance. Obviously, these assault troops would have been raised to a fever pitch by their commanders, since this was to be the first American landing against a defended shore in the European theatre. One would expect such men to be eager to leave the landing craft under any circumstances—unless it was obvious that the enemy was not resisting elsewhere, and a safer point of egress could therefore be found. It is curious also that the troops "refused" to leave the boat, meaning not only that they declined to obey the commander of the ves-

---

[142] Memorandum from T.B. Brittain, commanding USS MONROVIA to Commander-in-Chief, United States Fleet, Subject: Report of Operations in Connection with Amphibious Phase of HUSKY, July 10-12, 1943, p. 1, USMC Collection, Box 116, File No. 5.

[143] *Ibid.*, p. 2.

[144] *Ibid.*, p. 3.

---

[145] *Ibid.*, pp. 3-6.

[146] *Ibid.*, p. 4.

sel, namely McMonagle, but also that they remained recalcitrant in the face of an order from the man in charge of the party, whether he was a commissioned or non-commissioned officer. It is, of course, unthinkable that the man in command of such a landing party would be in any way implicated in such a refusal to disembark. Finally, it is noteworthy that Brittain, in his report of the incident, does not call for an investigation of its circumstances and the punishment of the perpetrators. Surely some punishable offense---cowardice in the face of the enemy, insubordination, dereliction of duty all come to mind---was at least arguably committed by someone on Boat 31. It therefore seems odd that Brittain did not seek charges against men who apparently failed to obey their orders after McMonagle had been wounded obeying his.

C.W. Harwood, a Captain in the U.S. Coast Guard, commanded the USS *Joseph T. Dickman*, as well as a task group consisting of the *Dickman*, HMS *Prince Charles* and HMS *Prince Leopold*, both of the Royal Navy, and a small fleet of landing craft. Harwood's group had the task of landing 1st Ranger Battalion, 4th Ranger Battalion, 1st Battalion 39th Engineers and 83d Chemical Warfare Battalion on the beach at Gela on July 10. The group encountered heavy weather during the day of July 9, 1943. While these conditions did not directly affect the *Dickman* or its landing craft, it may have indirectly affected the course of the invasion in the Gela area by delaying the arrival of two of the group's control ships. [147]

The *Dickman* group approached the beach at Gela safely and surely through the use of a submarine beacon. After experiencing some difficulty in obtaining an accurate reading of its position relative to the shore, the *Dickman* launched a marking boat which found and marked the center of the beach. *Dickman* began lowering landing boats at 12:45 AM. There were thirty such boats in all; twenty-six had been preloaded with troops before being lowered, while the remaining four boats, preloaded with equipment only, received their troops by means of nets over the ship's side. The *Dickman* completed lowering the landing boats at 1:25 AM. Captain Harwood then held the boats nearby while he awaited the arrival of the primary and secondary control boats. After waiting unsuccessfully for another thirty minutes, Harwood directed the boats to proceed without the control ships. [148]

Fortunately, the control boats arrived as the landing vessels moved toward the shore. As a result, all of the boats landed on the correct beach, but were thirty minutes behind schedule. The enemy greeted the boats with some machine gun fire, as well as with light cannon fire. Casualties among the boat crews included five wounded and one killed. An Army officer was also killed while still aboard his landing boat. In general, however, the troops crossed the beach without suffering many casualties. The enemy directed its fire at the boats, and at least two of them were damaged. Support boats silenced many of the enemy weapons by firing rockets. [149]

The *Dickman* and its landing boats began unloading on July 10, and continued until they were finished at 8:00 PM on the next day. The enemy subjected the *Dickman* to assault from the air on the morning of 11 July. This attack was without effect, but the enemy launched another such attack at about 4:00 PM on the same day, using a large formation of bombers. The *Dickman* suffered some superficial damage from this bombing attack, and six of her crew were slightly wounded. There was yet a third attack by enemy aircraft approximately forty minutes later, but no bombs were dropped near the *Dickman*. However, a nearby transport vessel, the SS *Robert Rowan*, was struck by at least one enemy bomb and caught fire. The *Dickman* took aboard 92 survivors before the *Robert Rowan* exploded. One of the *Dickman's* landing boats shot down an enemy fighter plane near the beach with its own machine guns. Despite this success, however, the repeated enemy air attacks led Harwood to the rather gloomy conclusion that "it is unlikely that a determined enemy plane assault could have been beaten off." [150]

Cruiser Division Thirteen spent an eventful five days during the assault phase of the invasion of Sicily. The Division formed a part of a Cover and Support Group for the JOSS attack force which assaulted the southern coast of Sicily in the Gela-Licata area. The Group comprised Cruiser Division Thirteen, including the cruisers *Brooklyn* and *Birmingham*, as well as Destroyer Squadron Thirteen, which consisted of the destroyers *Buck, Roe, Swanson, Nicholson, Ludlow, Woolsey, Wilkes, Bristol* and *Edison*. L. T. DuBose commanded the Group from his flagship, the cruiser *Brooklyn*. [151]

---

[147] Memorandum from Captain C.W. Harwood, U.S.C.G., Commanding Officer, USS *Joseph T. Dickman* to Commander-in-Chief, United States Fleet dated 13 July 1943, Subject: Report of Operation HUSKY—July 1-12, 1943, p. 1, USMC Collection, Box 116, File No. 7.

[148] *Ibid.*
[149] *Ibid.*, p. 2.
[150] *Ibid.*, pp. 2-3.
[151] Memorandum from L.T. DuBose, Commander Cruiser Division Thirteen, to Commander-in-Chief, United States Fleet dated July 23, 1943, Subject: Action Report, 10-14 July

DuBose's Group made its approach to Licata without incident. Shortly after 2:00 AM on July 10 the several ships in the Group took their stations for close fire support along the coast before Licata. At about 3:00 AM, however, the destroyers *Roe* and *Swanson* collided, resulting in serious damage to both vessels. DuBose directed them to proceed to Malta for repairs, and their places were taken by the *Buck* and *Ludlow*, which had previously been assigned to screen *Brooklyn* and *Birmingham*, respectively. [152]

Throughout the assault phase, the members of the Group had great difficulty in communicating with their individual shore fire control parties. Because of such a problem, the *Brooklyn* reverted to firing on prearranged targets, beginning at 4:42 AM and continuing until 5:20 AM. An unidentified enemy aircraft attacked the *Brooklyn* shortly after it had commenced firing, straddling it with two bombs. On this occasion, as on many others over the next four days, enemy aircraft approached without warning, having thwarted the ships' radar by flying at low level. The Group provided supporting fire during the first two hours after daylight. Although the cruisers were equipped with their own spotter aircraft, they were not provided with adequate cover by Allied fighter planes, and DuBose ordered their recall, fearing loss of both the aircraft and their pilots. In spite of this difficulty, at 8:05 AM the Italian flag was removed from the Castel St. Angelo above Licata, and the American flag hoisted up. About an hour later DuBose received an order to cease firing. [153]

The remainder of the Group's stay in the invasion zone was rather ordinary, but not without points of interest. On July 11 the *Birmingham* was assigned a fire support mission off Port Empedocle, while the rest of the Group patrolled in the landing area. The next day also passed without incident until shortly after 10:00 PM, when radar alerted the Group to the approach of hostile aircraft. The ships maneuvered independently, and a stick of bombs missed the *Brooklyn* by about 200 feet. For the next twenty minutes the enemy aircraft shadowed the *Brooklyn*, but did not again attack. The enemy again attacked the *Brooklyn* from the air on July 13, with the same lack of success. The rest of that day was spent patrolling and rendering fire support. On July 14 there was some excitement when first the *Woolsey* and then the *Brooklyn* each detonated a mine. In neither case, however, was the damage more than superficial, and by 2:45 PM Cruiser Division Thirteen was on its way

to Algiers for fuel and ammunition. [154]

The destroyer USS *Mervine*, under the command of D.R. Frakes, sailed from Oran during the afternoon of July 5, 1943 as a part of Task Force 85 escorting a convoy to the theatre of operations for the invasion of Sicily. The *Mervine* did not encounter the enemy during this voyage, but did experience rough seas on the afternoon of July 9, and a wind of force four from the Northwest. [155]

The wind and sea in the assault area became calm after sunset. Between approximately 10:30 PM on July 9 and 2:00 AM on July 10, the *Mervine* observed flares, searchlights and heavy anti-aircraft fire behind the beaches in the vicinity of Gela. At 3:10 AM the first wave of landing boats started for GREEN 2 Beach at a speed of six knots. At 3:48 AM the *Mervine* began firing on an entire series of prearranged targets, and continued to do so until 4:17 AM. Between 4:30 AM and about 5:07 AM, enemy aircraft attacked several nearby ships with bombs, and the *Mervine* was able to take one of them, a twin-engined German bomber, under fire, albeit unsuccessfully. The *Mervine*'s captain was proud to report, however, that while neighboring vessels continued to fire at covering Spitfires "throughout the day," believing them to be enemy aircraft, his own crew refrained from such a potentially egregious error. The *Mervine*'s forbearance on this account, Frakes admitted, was due to the fact that the ship had received an officer specially trained in aircraft recognition on leaving the U.S. [156]

The *Mervine* was able to establish communications with its Shore Fire Control Party shortly after 6:00 AM, and thereafter destroyed an enemy gun emplacement which had been firing on the beaches. However, this was the last opportunity for the . to fire its guns. There were no further requests for fire support, and at 2:30 PM the . was attached to the anti-submarine screen, and stayed with it until it left the invasion area on July 13. [157]

Task Force Eighty-Five, also identified as the CENT Attack Force, included the destroyer USS *Beatty*, commanded by Commander Frederick C. Stelter, Jr. The task force assembled off the isle of Gozo on July 9, and began its approach to Sicily. Like her sister vessels, the *Beatty* encountered, after 10:00 PM, increasingly favorable weather, with

1943, p. 1, USMC Collection, Box 117, File No. 29.

[152]   *Ibid.*, pp. 1-2.
[153]   *Ibid.*, pp. 2-3.

[154]   *Ibid.*, pp. 3-5.
[155]   Memorandum from D.R. Frakes, Commanding Officer, USS *Mervine*, to Commander-in-Chief, United States Fleet, dated July 15, 1943, Subject: Assault against Scoglitti, Sicily, on July 10, 1943, p. 1, USMC Collection, Box 117, File No. 28.
[156]   *Ibid.*, pp. 1-4.
[157]   *Ibid.*, p. 3.

cloudless skies, force one winds from the Northwest, and calm seas. These conditions obtained until at least first light. Shortly after 11:30 PM the crew of the *Beatty* first sighted transport planes when five of them passed close by at an altitude of about 100-200 feet. [158]

At about 10:40 PM anti-aircraft fire began around Gela and several other areas in the CENT-DIME zone. The fire was quite intense and continued so until after midnight, when it became more scattered. The enemy were also observed using flares to advantage, especially against aircraft dropping paratroops. The crew of the *Beatty* began observing aircraft falling from the sky in flames at 11:25 PM. [159]

On arrival in the invasion area, the *Beatty* undertook screening operations with the transport ships until the latter were in their anchorage area, and then took her station as part of a fire support group in the CENT-DIME zone. While the *Beatty* and her cohorts awaited the departure of the first wave of invasion troops, the entire force was illuminated by two searchlights located on the beach. The lights were eventually shot out, having caused the fire support group great consternation, though little damage. [160]

Although the transports to which the *Beatty* was assigned were originally scheduled to depart for the beach at 1:51 AM, in fact they did not do so until 3:42 AM, apparently because some of the landing boats could not be made ready in a timely fashion. At 4:07 AM one of the landing craft requested the *Beatty* and another destroyer, the USS *Cowie*, to open fire. The two ships then fired on the landing zone for a period of six minutes, covering it with a hail of projectiles. After completing this task, the *Beatty* took up anti-aircraft/anti-submarine patrol while it awaited contact with the shore fire control party. At 4:20 AM the *Beatty* and other vessels in the vicinity came under air attack by aircraft that could not be seen and were undetectable by radar, because of their low approach. The enemy scored no hits. [161]

First light occurred at 4:01 AM, inaugurating a day of tension, anxiety and intense activity for the crew of the *Beatty* and her neighboring ships. About an hour and a quarter later, two bombs from enemy aircraft landed in the water, the first 2000 yards from the *Beatty*'s starboard beam, and the second at approximately the same distance from her starboard

bow. At 8:30 AM the *Beatty* managed to contact its Shore Fire Control Team, attached to the 2d Battalion, 180th Regimental Combat Team, which reported that the landing was successful, good progress was being made, and that fire support was not yet needed. Thereafter, the activity of enemy aircraft was almost continuous. Stelter reported that hostile planes would appear at the beachhead flying low and fast from overland to strafe and bomb the invasion troops and then disappear. The commanding officer of the *Beatty* went so far as to say that:

> They maintained their nuisance value the entire period of daylight, usually appeared in the temporary absence of our fighters and in general gave an excellent account of themselves.

The reason for the success of the enemy fighters was that because of their low altitude, the ships could not fire on them with impunity, for fear of injuring Allied troops. At the same time, Allied fighters would not follow the enemy down, because when they did so, they too were fired on by small craft and beach parties. At midmorning the 20mm cannon of the *Beatty* contributed to the destruction of one enemy plane which crashed inland after running the gauntlet of shipboard batteries. At 10:46 AM, however, the *Beatty*'s crew misidentified a P-51 as an FW 190 and discharged a barrage of machine gun, 20mm and 40mm fire at it, luckily without effect. Stelter characterized the incident as "excusable," in view of the crew's state of anxiety, and the fact that the enemy aircraft were "going about their business with no air opposition." [162]

Air activity continued around the *Beatty* after noon. The crew observed two FW 190s shoot down an Allied plane Southeast of Scoglitti at about 1:15 PM. Two hours later, Stelter observed enemy bombers over the DIME sector, as well as a Ju-88 above the transport area, apparently on a reconnaissance mission. Allied fighters did not intervene in either case. The enemy bombed the beach in the DIME sector at 5:35 PM, and at 6:47 PM the crews of several LCTs fired on friendly aircraft. Finally, between 8:40 and 9:00 PM a very heavy enemy bomb landed in the water quite close to the *Beatty*, shaking her "considerably," and two aircraft fell in flames behind the beach. As darkness approached, Stelter could see twelve distinct fires ashore in the CENT area, caused by heavy gunfire from ships, small craft and shore parties. [163]

An hour after sunrise on July 11 the *Beatty* fired

---

[158]  Memorandum from Frederick C. Stelter, Jr., Commanding Officer, USS BEATTY, to Commander-in-Chief, United States Fleet, dated July 15, 1943, Subject: Report of Action—Operation HUSKY, p. 1, USMC Collection, Box 116, File No. 15.

[159]  *Ibid.*

[160]  *Ibid.*, p. 2.

[161]  *Ibid.*, pp. 2-3.

[162]  *Ibid.*, pp. 3-4.

[163]  *Ibid.*, pp. 4-5.

on a low flying Me 110 that was retiring at high speed from a bombing attack in the DIME sector. Although the plane was under heavy fire from other ships as well, it managed to escape overland without damage. Thereafter, the *Beatty* fired its cannon almost continuously for over three hours at pre-designated targets ashore, under the direction of the Shore Fire Control Party. During this sequence, Stelter's vessel fired 799 rounds, and was forced to cease firing because of the depletion of its ammunition supply. The *Beatty* took station in an anti-submarine screen at 11:40 AM, having been relieved by the USS *Lamb*. [164]

At 7:00 PM the *Beatty* moved south of Scoglitti, taking up an anti-aircraft/anti-submarine patrol while it awaited formation of a convoy to which it had been assigned. Between 10:30 and midnight, the surrounding area was alive with gunfire from both ships and the beaches. Flares illuminated the transports just off shore, their effect being enhanced by a cloudless sky, a half moon, and the dark background along the beaches. During this period, Stelter observed at least ten aircraft crash into the sea in flames. Then, at about 10:45 PM, the crew of the *Beatty* heard an aircraft approaching the ship's starboard bow out of the dark over the beach from Scoglitti. The aircraft could not be seen, and appeared to be making an unusual amount of noise. Simultaneously, fragments from a five inch shell, fired at the plane by another ship, struck the *Beatty* on its starboard side, after the shell detonated on impact in the water nearby. The aircraft then flashed across the bow of the *Beatty* at a height of about forty feet, narrowly missing the forecastle, and crashing in the water about fifty feet from the ship. During the plane's passage through the *Beatty*'s line of fire, the vessel's 20mm battery managed to fire sixty rounds at it, before it was identified as a C-47. Fortunately, the *Beatty* was able to rescue the aircraft's crew intact. It had already dropped its cargo of paratroops, in spite of a gauntlet of fire thrown up by both friend and foe. [165]

A glimpse into the hazards that might have confronted the HUSKY invasion force, particularly if the obvious landing beaches had been manned by a resolute and well-equipped foe, can be obtained by considering the experience of the USS *Frederick Funston* and her crew. The *Funston* was a combat loader and carried 2,000 troops of the 45th Infantry Division to the invasion zone, about six miles northwest of Scoglitti. The *Funston* arrived at its destination at about 11:00 PM on July 9, 1943, and began launching landing craft and support boats at about 12:30 AM on July 10. Thereafter, the crew worked continuously

without respite at the task of unloading troops, supplies and equipment, until at 6:00 PM on July 13 the *Funston* departed from its position in the invasion area, having set a course for the naval base at Oran. [166]

Although the *Funston* completed its assigned mission, and did so with dispatch and without damage to itself or its crew, nevertheless there occurred a number of misadventures and incidents that highlighted the potential for catastrophe present in the HUSKY operation. For example, the *Funston* possessed sixteen landing and support boats, no less than twelve of which were stranded ashore during the operation and had to be rescued by the ship's salvage party. As the *Funston*'s commanding officer reported, the loss of these boats "was a prime factor in delaying vital supplies to the landed and engaged troops." One reason for this situation was the deplorable condition of the beach, the surface of which was rough and incredibly uneven for hundreds of feet out to sea. In addition, the surf was very bad, so that many landing craft broached or sank after having made only one or two trips to the beach. Inability to handle the surf was in turn due to lack of skill on the part of landing craft personnel, as well as to shortcomings in their equipment, which was underpowered and difficult to handle. [167]

The *Funston*'s commanding officer generally praised the men under his command, saying that "the behavior under fire, the untiring work in unloading for a continuous sixty hour period, the determined spirit to get the job done in the shortest possible time displayed by all hands was of the very highest caliber." He also said that "[T]here was observed not a single case of hesitation or reticence in the performance of any task, regardless of existing conditions of war or battle." [168]

In spite of the tenor of these remarks, however, the *Funston*'s captain, J.E. Murphy, felt compelled to disclose the darker side of the experience. The more questionable actions of the men under Murphy's command occurred on the beach, and included what Murphy termed "cases... of culpable inefficiency and neglect of duty." Murphy described encountering landing craft fully loaded with "such vital supplies as ammunition" abandoned by their crews on the beach. Evidently, there had been a delay in unloading by the shore parties, and the boat crew had simply "wandered off " rather than commence unloading on their

---

[164]   *Ibid.*, pp. 5-6.
[165]   *Ibid.*, pp. 6-7.

[166]   Memorandum from J. E. Murphy, Commanding Officer, USS *Frederick Funston*, to Commanding Officer, United States Fleet, dated July 16, 1943, Subject: Report of Operation HUSKY, p. 1, USMC Collection, Box 116, File No. 6.
[167]   *Ibid.*, p. 3.
[168]   *Ibid.*, p. 5.

own. Murphy also found that other boats, stranded by the low tide, had been abandoned by their crews. The same boats were later easily rescued under their own power at higher tide by salvage parties. In still other cases, boats that had been sunk or stranded were retrieved by the salvage crews, following which the assigned boat crew would appear as if by magic to take over the vessel, having observed the rescue from the safety of a nearby trench. Murphy was distressed and frustrated by such conduct.

It seemed to be "the thing to do" to some crews when a little difficulty with their boat was had, to dismount the machine guns, set them up inland and "pot shot" at passing enemy planes of which there were considerable during the first two days. Those things reflect on the basic selection and/or training of these crews; something that the ship's officers in their short period of association and intensive training with these crews cannot overcome. Unfortunately, the above described cases could not be identified with the guilty personnel due to the other numerous and vital activities going on. [169]

The reports of the *Funston*'s landing boat officers accompanied that of Murphy, and are equally revealing about the details of the actual assault landing itself. For example, Ensign R.R. Groves reported that on July 10, 1943 he was ordered to "ride to the line of departure" on board the Primary Control Vessel of the USS *Calvert*. The *Funtson*'s boats were carrying a large number of troops and supplies from the nearby *Calvert*; the "Primary Control Vessel" was a boat detailed to each transport ship for the purpose of controlling the progress of the assault craft. When Groves and the Primary Control Vessel arrived at the line, the Ensign found that "[T[hings... were very ragged."

The control vessel received orders to leave for the beach before the first four waves were formed. After going approximately eight hundred yards orders were received to report back to the *Calvert*. Word was passed over the P.A. system and a wide turn was made and the boats led back to the rendezvous area. When the waves were again almost formed, the officer in charge issued orders for all boats to report back to the *Calvert*. Just after this word was passed the *Calvert*'s Boat

Group Commander came alongside saying shove off for the beach; therefore boats were going both ways.

Although the boats to which Groves was assigned eventually made it to the beach in good order, the situation continued to be difficult. Because of the rough condition of the beach, compounded by the surf, better than half of the assault boats were encountering difficulty in retracting. Even worse, when Groves' vessel landed, it picked up men from the *Calvert* and another ship, the USS *Arundel*. From these men Groves discovered that the assault boats were all landing on the wrong beach. From that point forward Groves directed the incoming boats to the "new beach," only to find that it was not correctly marked. Groves observed that the traffic control boat assigned to this beach was "never seen," and that those on the beach offered very little help in either unloading or getting boats off the beach. [170]

One of Groves' colleagues, Ensign O.J. Barr, departed with him from the *Funston* at 12:30 AM on July 10 and went at once to PC-542, the control vessel for the *Calvert*. After Groves had debarked, the crew of the control vessel told Barr that the *Calvert*'s Scout Boat, with which Barr and his boat were to rendezvous, had left for the beach an hour before. Barr then searched for the Scout Boat of another transport, the USS *Neville*, but failed to locate it. Barr patrolled in toward the shore, until about 2:30 AM, when he encountered the *Neville*'s Scout Boat. Together, they searched another half hour for the *Calvert*'s Scout Boat, without success. The two craft then separated, but the *Neville*'s Scout reappeared a few minutes later, leading two waves of assault craft toward the beach. Enemy resistance was light, no shots were fired at Barr's boat, and after first light he was able to move ashore and assist in marking the beach. [171]

Ensign Barr's boat thus apparently failed in its mission, through no fault of its crew and commander, but rather as the result of the confusion that evidently reigned in the sector. Barr and his charge transferred supplies from the *Funston* to shore on July 11 and 12; on the following two days the ensign went aboard the *Funston* to assist in unloading her holds. When his ship returned to base, Barr reported to his commanding officer that in his opinion the

[169]   *Ibid.*, pp. 4-5.

[170]   *Ibid.*; enclosure A to memorandum of J. E. Murphy; memorandum from Ensign R.R. Groves, Boat Group Commander, to the Commanding Officer, J.E. Murphy, July 15, 1943, p.1.

[171]   *Ibid.*; enclosure A to memorandum of J.E. Murphy; memorandum from Ensign O.J. Barr, Boat Officer, to the Commanding Officer, J.E. Murphy, July 15, 1943, p. 1.

beaches to which the *Calvert* and *Neville* had been assigned were "absolutely unfit" for operations by LCVs, particularly because of a shallow sand bar that paralleled the beach for miles at distances from 10 to 150 yards offshore. This sand bar, and the running surf, swamped and broached "numerous" LCVs. As to the boats which made it ashore, many of them remained "sitting... waiting to be unloaded," in part because the shore party was undermanned, but also because of poor marking of the beach, clogging of the beach with boats that were unable to retract, and lack of proper traffic control. All of this was exacerbated by the unwillingness of boat crews to tow, and thus salvage, boats that had been broached. Barr reported making seven trips to the beach, during all of which time he never observed a boat in trouble being towed by one of her sister craft. [172]

Another boat officer from the *Funston*, Ensign J.W. Auter, was assigned to the *Calvert* on D-day, and had a similarly disquieting experience. Auter made three trips to the beach on July 10, and on the remaining days stayed aboard the *Funston* working with repair crews and unloading supplies. The Ensign boarded the *Calvert* at 1:00 AM on July 10, only to be informed that the boats from the first wave, to which he was attached, had already been lowered into the water and were forming a rendezvous circle. Auter then made an unsuccessful attempt to obtain orders for alternative action, and then accompanied another officer in one of the sixth wave boats. When they reached their rendezvous circle, however, they found that the first four waves had left the area, and that the remaining boats were "moving in disorderly circles, apparently without definite orders or purpose." Again, because Auter and the other officers had not been given alternative orders, a long period of time passed, and the disarray continued, until orders were received directing the boats to form waves astern the secondary control vessel. [173]

Auter's first trip to the beach was "equally disorderly." In general, the boats involved did not form waves or maintain station. The boat that Auter was in had difficulty from the start as a result of poor loading; the vessel was too heavy in the bow and listed to starboard, and as a result was swamped. The boat hit a sand bar about 50 yards from shore, and because of its condition, the crew had to drive it through the sand to the beach, even though they knew this would mean that the boat could not be retracted. Auter found the beach itself to be "very

difficult" because of high surf and the lack of necessary markings. Auter reported that these factors, as well as the unseaworthiness of fully loaded LCVs in moderately heavy seas, contributed to the great number of boats left abandoned on the beach. The most important element, however, seems to have been the "*slowness of soldiers* leaving the boats," which caused the ramp to be in the water longer than necessary, with the result that the boats were filled with water. [174]

The experience of Ensign S.E. Frank, another boat officer on board the *Funston* and detailed for work on the *Calvert*, illustrates the tenuous nature of the HUSKY undertaking. Frank reported that after going aboard his assault craft at 3:00 AM, he encountered "much difficulty" in the rendezvous area. The rendezvous circles were not well ordered, in part because the fifth, sixth and seventh waves were "broken," and the primary control vessel repeatedly left the area in which it was supposed to be. After cobbling together a makeshift wave from assault craft left behind by the first four waves, Frank followed the secondary control boat to the departure line. There, he was once again delayed by the many boats broached on the sand bar. Although Frank should have had a scout and raider boat to guide his wave to the shore, he did not see them during the entire operation. As a result of all of this, it was 5:30 AM and light before Frank and his wave hit the beach, thankfully without opposition. Frank reported that the beach party had not properly marked the beach. He also gave his opinion that the many boats lost on the beach resulted from four factors, namely (1) the absence of adequate help to unload the landing craft; (2) overloading of assault vessels; (3) the lowering of the vessel's ramp before help was available to unload; and (4) the failure to test motor vehicles before loading them in assault craft, with a view to having some assurance that the vehicles would start once on the beach. [175]

Another combat loader engaged in the Sicily operation was the USS *Ann Arundel*, commanded by L.Y. Mason, Jr. It arrived on station off the coast of Sicily at approximately 11: 45 PM on July 9, 1943, along with the USS *Neville* and other vessels in the attack force. Within a few hours it had all of its boats in the water, and began disembarking troops and high priority cargo at shortly after 7:00 AM. It began a shuttle to "*Neville* Red Beach" that continued almost without interruption thereafter, night and day,

---

[172] *Ibid.,* pp. 1-2.
[173] *Ibid;* enclosure A to memorandum of J.E. Murphy; memorandum from Ensign J.W. Auter, Boat Officer, to the Commanding Officer, J.E. Murphy, July 15, 1943, p. 1.
[174] *Ibid.,* pp. 1-2.
[175] *Ibid.;* enclosure A to memorandum of J.E. Murphy; memorandum from Ensign S.E. Frank, Boat Officer, to the Commanding Officer, J.E. Murphy, July 16, 1943, pp. 1-2.

until the ship's mission was completed. All of this did not occur without incident. The *Arundel* experienced numerous bombing attacks, and at one point all of its LCVPs were stranded on the beach, apparently because of congestion and slower unloading caused by the large volume of package cargo then being deposited ashore. The ship's captain also reported a distinctly disconcerting incident that occurred at 10:30 PM on July 11, when a "considerable" flight of aircraft was in the area. These included both friends (transports with paratroops) and foe, the latter dropping both bombs and flares. As a result of the enemy presence, however, there was "a very considerable volume of fire...put up by the transports." Mason estimated that at least five aircraft were shot down, it being impossible to determine their origin. [176] The *Arundel* sailed from Sicilian waters at about 5:15 PM on July 13, having successfully completed her mission, without substantial damage to the vessel or injury to her crew.

One officer who had an opportunity to observe and comment upon the landing phase of the Sicily invasion in the sector of the 45th Infantry Division was W.B. Phillips, the Commander of Transports, Amphibious Force, U.S. Atlantic Fleet. Phillips had his headquarters on the USS *Ancon,* from which he directed twenty-one additional transport vessels divided into four divisions. One of these, the Third Division, comprised of eight vessels, departed for North Africa on May 10, 1943 with a full complement of invasion troops. The remaining three divisions stayed in the Chesapeake Bay region for additional training without troops. Final embarkation took place between May 24 and June 7, and on the following day the three divisions formed a convoy and departed for Oran, Algeria, where it arrived on June 22. [177]

The period between June 22 and July 4 was spent in intensive preparation for the coming invasion. These preliminaries included "a complete rehearsal landing" on the night of June 24-25 and a joint Army/Navy conference on board the USS *Leonard Wood* on July 3, at which the entire operation was given a detailed review. Two days later three of the transport divisions left Oran in the company of ten additional control vessels and made their way with-

out incident to the waters south of Malta. Finally, at 6:00 PM on July 9 the transport vessels under Phillips' command began their final approach to Sicily from the area southwest of Malta. Transports, escorts and control vessels of the so-called DIME task force were in the lead, while those in the CENT task force followed. [178]

Phillips' convoy ran a parallel course to that taken by a convoy of the British BARK force. The seas in the approach lanes thus became rather crowded. At about 6:15 PM the CENT and DIME forces deployed into five columns of ships, and about an hour and a quarter later the convoy, its escorts and the control vessels passed the Gozo Island lighthouse inbound for Sicily. However, the wind had begun to blow at about 35 knots, kicking up a moderate sea and swell, so that it began to appear that a successful landing could not be made. For an hour or more, the convoy maneuvered at 50 degree turns in order to avoid other convoys in the crowded and rough seas. By about 9:30 PM, however, the seas had settled enough to permit the convoy to undertake its final approach course. As the approach continued, Phillips observed intermittent gunfire ahead and on both bows, as well as several flares dropped by enemy aircraft near the beach. [179]

According to the plan under which Phillips and his convoy were operating, the disembarkation phase of the assault was to begin at 2:45 AM on July 10. The operational plan, however, was based on the assumption that the landing force would arrive in the so called Transport Area at least three and one-half hours prior to disembarkation. This would permit the force two and one-half hours to get out the landing boats and load and assemble the four assault waves, plus another fifty-eight minutes to make the 10,000 yard run to the beach. The last assault transport, the USS *Neville,* did not arrive in the Transport Area until fifteen minutes past midnight. The net effect of this was that the convoy would have at least an hour less time to work with in order to meet its established deadline. This situation was not made better by the fact that the moderate sea and swell which was now being encountered was slowing down the debarkation of troops, vehicles and equipment from the assault transports. Moreover, the convoy was observing large fires ashore, a powerful searchlight in operation, and anti-aircraft fire at various locations on the beaches. In view of this, the task force commander extended H-hour for a period of one hour to 3:45 AM. [180]

[176] Memorandum from L.Y. Mason, Jr., Commanding Officer, USS ANNE ARUNDEL, to Commander-in-Chief, U.S. Fleet, dated July 17, 1943; Subject: Action Report; Operation HUSKY, pp. 1-9, USMC Collection, Box 116, File No. 8.

[177] Memorandum from W.B. Phillips, Commander Transports, Amphibious Force, U.S. Atlantic Fleet, dated July 17, 1943; Subject: Operation HUSKY—Report of; pp. 1-2; USMC Collection, Box 117, file No. 18.

[178] *Ibid.,* pp. 2-3.
[179] *Ibid.,* p. 3.
[180] *Ibid.,* pp. 4-5.

It may have been this delay in getting off the mark which ultimately caused the confusion that infected the American beaches. At 2:45 AM the USS *Leonard Wood's* control vessel set off for its line of departure for YELLOW beach with its first four assault waves. Eighteen minutes later the control vessel for the USS *Florence Nightingale* left for the GREEN beach departure line, likewise with four assault waves. At about the same time respective control vessels for the *Neville* and *Calvert* left for the RED beach departure line. Assault boats from the *Florence Nightingale* and the *Leonard Wood* set off for the beach at about 3:36 AM. As a result of an erroneous calculation of their starting position, however, the assault boats from the *Florence Nightingale* landed not on GREEN beach, as intended, but on YELLOW beach instead. Course corrections were made to allow other boats from the *Florence Nightingale* to land nearer GREEN beach. [181]

Cover fire on beaches GREEN and YELLOW was provided by the destroyers USS *Tillman* and *Knight*, which commenced firing at 3:30 AM. Additional support was provided by eight support boats which accompanied the first four assault waves from the *Leonard Wood* and the *Florence Nightingale*. These support boats laid down a "very effective" rocket barrage as the first waves from each ship were about one thousand yards from the beach. The landing of the first four assault waves was thus an overall success, even though eight special beach marking scout boats that had been assigned to mark RED, GREEN and YELLOW beaches were "never seen" by the assault boats and their control vessels, leading Phillips to conclude that the scout boats "had not proved of any advantage." Nevertheless, the fifth, sixth and seventh assault waves appear to have gotten to the beach without mishap, and most of the assault craft were successfully recovered, even though the surf was running at four to six feet. [182]

At about 6:00 AM the transport vessels began to move to inshore anchorages, after which they began to debark vehicles, equipment and supplies. This procedure continued throughout the morning. By 10:00 AM, however, it became apparent that the unloading process was in trouble, chiefly because of the stranding of the ships' boats on the beach. Phillips assigned blame for this condition to the inexperience of the crews, the high surf and the inability of the shore party to unload the boats promptly. Organized salvage parties were active on GREEN and YELLOW beaches, "but the rate of stranding exceeded their ef-

forts." [183]

An inspection party arrived at GREEN and YELLOW beaches at 3:00 PM to assess the situation. In addition to the surf running at 4 to 6 feet high, they discovered a very small gradient which forced the boats to make the final landing at low speed. This rendered the boats vulnerable to broaching unless they were unloaded and retracted promptly. Out of a total of 157 boats from Transport Division One, 76 were stranded, some containing vehicles which could not be unloaded. The beaches were improperly marked, and the party could only find the Beachmaster with difficulty. The beach parties were not coaching boats into proper landing places. Salvage boats were available off the beach, but no one from the beach party was there to direct them. At 5:30 PM a pontoon causeway being used to unload on GREEN beach began breaking up, and unloading was stopped. [184]

Because of the problems being encountered on YELLOW and GREEN beaches, an effort was made to locate landing beaches for LSTs where pontoons would not be necessary. This attempt failed, as did an investigation of Scoglitti harbor, which was found to be suitable for unloading only amphibious DUKWs. At 6:25 PM the officer in charge of the transports directed officers and boat crews to stand by their stranded boats for the purpose of assisting salvage parties. The transport commander also ordered each transport ship to send its own salvage party to the troubled beaches. In spite of all this, an attempt was made to continue unloading throughout the night, but this was hampered by the lack of available boats and "the inability of the Shore Parties to unload the boats." Flares and bombs being dropped by Axis forces also hampered the operation. [185]

By mid-morning of the next day, July 11, the operational staff had reached the point where it could no longer tolerate the situation on shore, and ordered that YELLOW, GREEN and RED beaches be relocated to an area just northwest of Scoglitti. Because some of the pontoon causeways on the original beaches were "well secured in place" and thus difficult to move, the LSTs continued to unload there. Phillips reported, however, that this decision did not retrieve the situation:

"The unloading conditions at the new beaches... were no better and possibly worse as far as landing boats were concerned as the old beaches. There were however exits for mov-

[181] *Ibid.*, pp. 5-6.
[182] *Ibid.*, p. 6.
[183] *Ibid.*, pp. 7-9.
[184] *Ibid.*, p. 9.
[185] *Ibid.*, p. 10.

ing Army equipment inshore at the new beaches. Boats were stranded rapidly on the new beaches, and the beaches became congested for unloading. The Shore and Beach Parties were scattered and uncertain of the location of the various beaches. After darkness loaded boats from the ships were being sent back." [186]

At 10:00 PM orders were issued to stop utilizing small boats for unloading during the night. These craft were to be loaded and ready to move ashore at daybreak. In any event, many of the small boats had returned from the beaches never having been unloaded in the first place. Nighttime unloading operations were confined to larger landing craft, but interruptions occurred as a result of aircraft, presumably of Axis origin, dropping flares and bombs. [187]

The passage of the night did not improve matters. During the night, at least one LST reported receiving no assistance in unloading. The task could only be accomplished with the aid of Seabees. The condition of the new beaches at daylight on July 12 was no better than it had been on the original beaches two days before. Phillips reported that:

"Stranded boats practically prevented the loaded boats from coming in and unloading. LCI(L)s were available for salvage work, but were not being properly used. Approximately forty small landing boats and 3 LCT(5)s were lying off the new beaches waiting to be unloaded. The unloading of the boats at the beaches at this time was being done mostly by ship's personnel instead of the Shore Party..." [188]

Despite its travail, Phillips' Transport Division One managed to be completely unloaded by 8:00 PM on July 12, with the exception of the USS *Alcyone*. The plight of the latter vessel induced an order requiring each other ship in the Division to send it a salvage party consisting of three men per boat stranded on the beach. Each salvage party included two officers. Transport Division One was not permitted to depart the landing zone until the *Alcyone* was completely unloaded. Because of the severity of the *Alcyone*'s situation, however, this order was changed, and the remaining ships in the Division formed a convoy, with nine escort destroyers, for Oran. The Division arrived at Oran without incident on July

15. [189]

The landing craft assigned to the transports under Phillips' command suffered heavy casualties in the invasion of Sicily. Phillips recited a litany of reasons for this outcome. Apart from the obvious physical causes, Phillips believed that his losses were caused by generally poor seamanship among the boat crews, which had been "turned out in mass production"; a tendency of officers to believe that a beach party would take care of their stranded boats, which led these officers to fail to make sufficient effort to help themselves; the fact that beach parties were composed of personnel who were not experienced seamen; poor discipline on the beach; and failure of the beach and shore parties to make use of available personnel. Phillips' recommended solution to this situation was to give command of the beach "from the high water mark to at least 100 yards inshore" to a Navy Captain "of great experience in seamanship," whose command would likewise be comprised of men with great experience at sea. [190]

Phillips' recommendations were generally supported by A. G. Kirk, Commander Sixth Amphibious Force, in his report on the HUSKY operation to the Commander in Chief, United States Fleet, dated September 13, 1943. On the subject of the training of boat crews, Kirk noted that the aim of the Amphibious Force was to supply trained crews for eight transport divisions. In view of the suddenness with which the HUSKY operation was laid on, however, he noted that it "is lucky that in this instance the requirements were for only four transport divisions." Kirk had strong words on the subject of the role of Army officers in the loading of transports bound for invasion deployment.

There is a general tendency on the part of the Army command thus far encountered to distrust AFAF Army Staff Officers and prefer their own. Enough qualified Transport Quartermasters must remain with the AFAF to keep the art of combat loading alive, and to permit early training of the Transport Quartermasters of the selected Army Division. There should be enough of them to permit adequate supervision of loading plans and actual loading sufficient to enable the Force Commander to actively control the actual loading in the light of his experience. The Army can no longer be permitted to combat load the ships of this Force, with no naval say so except as to stability. The Navy must re-

[186]  *Ibid.*
[187]  *Ibid.*
[188]  *Ibid.*, p. 11.

[189]  *Ibid.*, pp. 11-13.
[190]  *Ibid.*, pp. 18-19.

main in full control of all loading. [191]

L.B. Schulten, the Commanding Officer of the USS *Dorothea L. Dix*, one of the transports assigned to Task Unit 85.1.1, embarked with his ship from Newport News, Virginia on June 4, 1943. On board was the 2d Battalion of the 179th Regimental Combat Team, 45th Infantry Division. The *Dix* proceeded to Sicily and dropped anchor shortly after midnight on July 10, 1943 upon arrival at Transport Area One. Although the *Dix* had been unable to hoist out its landing craft on July 9, as originally planned, it nevertheless was able to place all of its boats in the water, in seaworthy condition, by about 3:45 AM on July 10. [192]

The *Dix* loaded out the 2d Battalion in 36 boats divided into four landing waves. There were no casualties among the nearly 1000 men who went ashore in these four waves and according to Schulten "[E]very wave hit the same and correct beach," namely GREEN Beach Western Section. All of Schulten's wave commanders complained of the inexperience of the boat crews, the inefficiency of the beach party, the slowness of the infantry to leave the boats, and the absence of salvage crews. [193]

The *Dix* managed to unload its troops, as well as a thousand tons of cargo and 180 vehicles, in slightly less than 48 hours. No fewer than 10 of its landing craft were lost on the beach, however, either as a result of being broached or flooded. Schulten believed that most of these were beyond salvaging. [194]

On August 5, 1943, R.L. Conolly, Commander of Task Force Eighty-six, provided the Commander in Chief, United States Fleet, with his narrative of events on the JOSS attack force, as well as his comments and recommendations. [195] Task Force 86 began its preparation and training for HUSKY at the Advanced Amphibious Bases in North African Waters in early April, 1943, even though it lacked its full complement of landing craft. Together with units of the U.S. 3d Infantry Division, the Task Force completed its final training, mounting and staging in the Bizerte-Tunis area. During this final training phase,

the Task Force practiced ship-to-shore movement, support boat and support wave procedure, pontoon drill, and individual task group and task force operations. During June, there were group exercises, a navigational problem and a full scale rehearsal employing the JOSS Army Assault Task Force. This final phase of training, particularly in the area of communications, was retarded by the very late arrival of much equipment and personnel from the United States, as well as the sinking of two LSTs, both loaded with equipment and stores. [196]

At the Advanced Amphibious Training Bases, all of the landing craft taking part in the operation were overhauled, altered and repaired as necessary. At the same time, these craft were used almost continuously for transferring of equipment and supplies to new bases at Bizerte and Tunis. Nevertheless, only one of the 275 landing craft and escorts assigned to proceed with the JOSS Attack Force failed to depart in convoy for Sicily because of mechanical failure. [197] In the event, 38 LSTs, 54 LCIs and 80 LCTs took part in the invasion with the JOSS Attack Force, along with an additional 24 British landing craft. [198]

Task Force 86 sailed for Sicily at about 9:00 AM on July 7, 1943. Apart from a variety of mechanical problems afflicting the landing craft, the transit to the assault area was uneventful. Late in the afternoon of July 9, however, the wind and sea became heavier, and although the Task Force's formation was in good order, it was strung out because LSTs were having difficulty making eight knots, LCIs were taking water and the smaller escort craft were struggling. Signaling to the smaller craft had become problematical. As a result, it was necessary for Conolly to "press the LSTs and LCIs during the Approach" in order to assure that the boats would be in position for the assault. Some of Conolly's LSTs had fallen so far behind that they lost sight of the other ships, became separated and failed to anchor in the proper transport areas. [199]

In addition to some of the LSTs, a number of the control ships acting as escorts for them became separated from the Task Force. The result of this was that these control vessels were not in their proper position in the assault rendezvous area to assemble and lead the assault LCVPs to the beach. In addition, the Task Force anchored farther out than the distance of 3.5 miles from the beach set forth in the plan. The cause of this was thought to be the fact that enemy searchlights constantly swept the approach area, giv-

---

[191] *Ibid*; memorandum from A.G. Kirk, Commander Sixth Amphibious Force, to Commander-in-Chief, United States Fleet, re: Commander Transports, Atlantic Fleet, Battle Report, HUSKY operation, September 13, 1943, pp. 1-3.

[192] Memorandum from L.B. Shelton, Commanding Officer, USS *Dorothea L. Dix*, to Commander-in-Chief, United States Fleet, dated July 17, 1943, Subject: Operation HUSKY, report of, p. 1; USMC Collection, Box 117, File No. 19.

[193] *Ibid.*, pp. 2-3.

[194] *Ibid.*, p. 7.

[195] Memorandum from R.L. Conolly, Commander Task Force 86 to Commander-in-Chief, United States Fleet, dated August 5, 1943, Subject: Action Reports and Comments on HUSKY; USMC Collection, Box 116, File No. 12.

[196] *Ibid.*, p. 9.

[197] *Ibid.*

[198] *Ibid.*, p. 10.

[199] *Ibid.*, pp. 11-14.

ing the false impression that the ships were closer than they actually were. The result was a much longer run for the assault LCVPs than had been planned. The longer run and the failure of some control ships to arrive in the rendezvous area caused the LCVPs to arrive at the beach late. [200]

In the assault area, Task Force 86 was aided by the HMS *Safari* and the USS *Bristol*, which braved enemy searchlights and the threat of gunfire to flash signals for the attack groups allotted to YELLOW and GREEN beaches. In fact, searchlights were an unnerving presence throughout the landing phase for Task Force 86. At 2:50 AM five shore searchlights illuminated the *Biscayne* and managed to keep their lights trained on her. In the early stages of the landing, searchlights illuminated not just the *Biscayne*, but BLUE and YELLOW beaches and other vessels as well. Nevertheless, the enemy held their fire, and indeed Conolly noted very little enemy gunfire on GREEN, YELLOW and BLUE beaches throughout the landing. [201]

All of the LCVPs in Task Force 86 were in the water by 2:52 AM, and the first two waves of them had landed on BLUE beach by 3:25 AM All was not without complication, however. Scout boats were only able to assist on YELLOW and GREEN beaches, although on the latter beach the scout did not arrive in time to mark for the first wave of LCVPs. On BLUE and RED beaches, however, there were no scout boats. These had been delayed in launching, and were further delayed by longer than anticipated approach runs. [202]

Beginning around 4:00 AM the enemy began to respond to the activities of Task Force 86 in earnest. Conolly observed "continuous artillery and heavy machine gun fire falling on Red Beach and approaches." Likewise, the first and second waves on BLUE beach received machine gun fire as well as attacks from enemy 75mm guns. At 4:30 AM the RED beach transport area came under heavy air attack. In the midst of all this, and in spite of the absence of some control boats and inadequate beach marking, most landing craft arrived on their beaches in good order. Further, the JOSS force did not experience the same salvage problem as those which overtook Task Force 85. Conolly reported that on all of the JOSS beaches, a total of only 10 landing craft proved to be unsalvageable. [203]

Shortly after 4:30 AM enemy aircraft dive bombed the *Biscayne*, but without success. During the next half hour, Conolly watched as the USS *Sentinel* was hit in another dive bombing attack. The HMS *Safari* and its escort were also attacked by enemy aircraft, but they escaped damage and were able to shoot down two of their assailants. Meanwhile, RED beach came under severe enemy artillery fire, so that an entire convoy of LCTs were instructed not to land as scheduled. This situation continued for almost two and a half hours, during which the Beachmaster on RED beach repeatedly warned away landing attempts because of the intensity of the enemy fire. Finally, the convoy of LCTs was ordered to land on RED beach "regardless of cost." This assault, supported by naval gunfire and smoke, carried the day, so that at about 8:00 AM "the situation on all beaches was satisfactory." All LSTs were then ordered to the beaches for unloading. [204]

The rest of July 10 passed in frenzied activity. While some landing craft continued to unload their cargoes at the beaches, other ships in Conolly's task force engaged ground targets near Licata in support of the troops now moving inland. At 10:30 AM the USS *Sentinel* capsized, finally going beneath the sea fifteen minutes later. At 11:00 AM Conolly received a report that 3rd Infantry Division had captured Licata. Within the hour, General Truscott had left the *Biscayne* for transport to Licata. By the evening, the Port of Licata had been opened, and control of unloading operations moved ashore. Conolly received an order to begin transferring landing craft for use in the DIME and CENT areas. [205]

Beginning at about 8:00 AM on July 11 all of the beaches in the *JOSS* area came under enemy dive bombing attack. One of Conolly's LSTs received a direct hit. Its load of ammunition and gasoline exploded on deck. Enemy air attacks were nearly continuous throughout the day, on both the beaches and the town of Licata. These attacks, however, were without further effect on Conolly's ships. Because of the ineffectiveness of the enemy assault, Task Force 86 was able to complete its task of unloading stores on July 12. In the evening of that day, it moved to the Gela area and dropped anchor. [206]

Captain R.A. Dierdorff, U.S. Navy, commanded the USS *Elizabeth C. Stanton* and Task Unit 81.2.3. The responsibility of his command was to deliver the 471 officers and 7500 men of 16th Regimental Combat Team to the beaches near Gela. These troops embarked at Algiers on July 6, 1943 and arrived on station shortly after midnight on July 10, after a passage marred by weather so severe that it was doubted

[200] *Ibid.*, p. 15.
[201] *Ibid.*, p. 16.
[202] *Ibid.*
[203] *Ibid.*, p. 17.

[204] *Ibid.*, pp. 17-19.
[205] *Ibid.*, pp. 20-22.
[206] *Ibid.*, pp. 22-27.

whether the invasion could be launched on schedule. However, the weather moderated upon arrival, and the group's beaches, designated RED-2 and GREEN-2, were promptly located by scout boats without detection or opposition. Assault waves from the transports in Dierdorff's command were promptly launched and began to arrive on schedule on the beaches.[207]

By 6:30 AM 16th Regimental Combat Team was reporting that it had successfully completed its landing. Despite this auspicious start for the day, however, it was in fact marked by vigorous enemy resistance. For while the Combat Team had successfully gotten itself ashore, Dierdorff's task unit was fully occupied during the next two days moving and unloading stores and equipment, activity which drew considerable attention on the part of the defenders. At midday there was fierce enemy shelling occurring on beach RED 2, and by late in the afternoon the beachmaster was warning against any further unloading of LSTs on beaches RED-2 and GREEN-2. Me-109s strafed and bombed both beaches at about 5:30 PM, setting on fire at least one LST at the cost of one fighter aircraft. The continuing shellfire convinced another of the task unit commanders that RED-2 and GREEN-2 were untenable.[208]

July 11 was no better. Shortly before 7:00 AM a force of about 12 Italian bombers attacked the transport area without casualties, in spite of very heavy antiaircraft fire. The enemy managed to set fire to the USS *Barnett*. Thirty minutes later Dierdorff received warning of another enemy air attack, and was ordered to proceed to seaward and maneuver independently to avoid damage. Toward midday a lone Me-109 bombed and strafed the beaches. Two hours later another swarm of enemy bombers appeared overhead, to be driven off without incident by Allied fighter aircraft. At 3:45 enemy fighter bombers again attacked the transport area, again without loss in spite of heavy antiaircraft fire from ships. The enemy managed to hit the *Robert Roland* in the vicinity of her no. 2 hatch, setting her afire. She blew up shortly after 5:00 PM and burned throughout the night. Attacks by enemy aircraft continued throughout the evening and night. Dierdorff's group finished unloading on July 12 and set sail for Algiers that evening.[209]

Captain Dierdorff's observations and recommen-

dations made subsequent to the operation are revealing. He offered, for example, detailed comments concerning the so-called Mark XIV sight mounted on anti-aircraft guns on the ships in his task unit. Although Dierdorff had been initially impressed by the performance of these gunsights on towed targets, he was disappointed in the results obtained by them in the Sicily operation. He observed that:

> Ships generally complained that this sight did not give sufficient lead on fast flying Me 109s over Transport Area. The *Betelgeuse*, which had marked success against Japanese planes at Guadalcanal without them, desires that hers be removed, and the former ring sight and tracer control be restored.[210]

Dierdorff also had comments concerning other equipment. Regarding the boats, the Captain referred particularly to the LCSS, noting that its rocket racks were "quite susceptible to damage when boats are being lowered or hoisted." He also complained that while all the other boats were diesel powered, this type had a gasoline engine, which required the storage of 5 gallon containers of fuel. And while the LCSS was rated for a speed of 16 knots, Dierdorff indicated that he had calibrated it to be capable of only 10.6 knots. Dierdorff also commented upon the performance of the LCVP. While this boat suffered from weakness in its rudder and steering gear, which caused them to be easily damaged and difficult to repair, Dierdorff had particular praise for the Gray Diesel Engines with which they were equipped, finding them "so outstandingly good that I believe the Gray people merit very definitely some special recognition for the excellence, both of design and workmanship. The engines are rugged, fool proof, and reliable, and are most satisfactory propulsion units."[211]

Noteworthy are Dierdorff's comments concerning communications. The Captain complained first about the so-called TBY radios, which were generally found to be unreliable. This was for the reason that atmospheric changes easily caused the sets to go off frequency, often requiring returning under adverse conditions. Further, because there were not enough regularly trained radio operators, reliance had to be placed on unskilled personnel for whom the equipment was too sophisticated. More importantly, Dierdorff criticized the communications plan for the operation. The Captain noted that the plan had failed

[207]  Memorandum from R.A. Dierdorff, Commander Task Unit 81.2.3 to Commander-in-Chief, United States Fleet, dated July 18, 1943, Subject: Report of Operations of Commander Task Unit 81.2.3 in landing Combat Team 16, U.S. Army, near Gela, Sicily, July 9-12, 1943; USMC Collection, Box 117, File No. 32, pp. 1-3.

[208]  *Ibid.*, pp. 8-9.

[209]  *Ibid.*, pp. 10-12.

[210]  *Ibid.*, Annex BAKER to Report of Operations of Commander Task Unit 81.2.3, p. 1.

[211]  *Ibid.*, p. 2.

to make clear whether routine reports on unloading, casualties and the like, should be transmitted in code or plain language. This resulted in such messages being sent both ways, thereby exposing the codes to compromise. Dierdorff particularly argued against the sending of reports regarding unloading and casualties in plain language, since such reports "are of vital concern to the enemy, enabling them to determine our losses, approximate time ships will be unloaded, and then make plans accordingly." He also called for "a workable system of air raid warning," namely a channel common to all vessels equipped with anti-aircraft weapons. Because such a system had been absent in the operation, Dierdorff's ships had fired on Allied aircraft because they had relied only on their own ships' lookouts for aircraft identification. [212]

Dierdorff commented that it had been " a distinct pleasure to operate in a Force in which a minimum of paternalistic supervision was imposed upon individual units," pointing out further that except for changes dictated by the tactical situation, " ships were permitted to work out their own salvation." He also observed that relations with the 16th Regimental Combat Team and its staff had been "very cordial," and that a spirit of teamwork had permeated at all levels between Army and Navy personnel. [213]

In the execution of the operation Dierdorff pointed out that the unloading of LSTs had been the major problem for his task unit. The LSTs had been afflicted with casualties to ramps, a gentle beach gradient which had required the use of pontoons, and the bombing, shelling and strafing of the beaches by the enemy. Nevertheless, he found that in general the LSTs had performed well. He had strong criticism, however, on the issue of fire discipline among anti-aircraft gunners in the task unit. Dierdorff particularly mentioned that the fire discipline of the smaller units was notoriously poor. They fired at anything with wings on it, within or out of range. Stray shots from an unknown source killed one man and wounded three in the *Betelgeuse* on the night of July 12th. The commanding officer and First Lieutenant of the *Thurston* were also wounded by a stray 20mm during the same attack.

Dierdorff believed that these dangerous deficiencies needed to be addressed during the training period prior to an amphibious operation during which all hands would take part in recognition drills coordinated by Navy and Army Air Force personnel and featuring the overflight of various Allied aircraft types at different altitudes and speeds. Dierdorff especially mentioned the problem of protecting beaches against "low-flying hedge-hopping fighter bombers." Since air cover was not an adequate solution to this problem, because of the tendency of naval gunners to fire at everything in the air, Dierdorff recommended the early use of barrage balloons and the immediate placement of anti-aircraft guns on the flanks of the beaches. [214]

Dierdorff's most serious concerns related to the problems encountered ashore. He noted, for example, that on the night of July 11-12 there were a number of broached and swamped boats on GREEN -2 and RED-2 beaches, resulting from the action of sea and wave and the "rather marked lack of Army assistance in unloading boats." More generally, the Captain made clear that in his view the central problem requiring "solution in the conduct of amphibious operations" was the unloading of boats at the beaches and the moving of the material unloaded to beach dumps. In Sicily, this problem was exacerbated by poor organization and execution. He illustrated this by the following commentary:

> Quite a number of landing boats were lost during the current operation almost solely because the Service Platoon of the Shore Party was either conspicuous by its absence, or present in inadequate strength properly and promptly to unload boats. This was especially true at night. As a result, boats' crews had the double duty of endeavoring to hold their boats on a shoal beach beset by sand bars and lashed by a considerable surf, and at the same time to unload them. All too often the boats broached or swamped in the process.

Dierdorff regarded this problem as so severe that he called for a joint Army and Navy Board to subject it to "the most rigorous examination" with a view to correction. [215]

Captain Dierdorff hammered on the significance of the unloading issue. His comments were acerbic. After excoriating the command system used for the unloading function, he suggested that

> While the problem could perhaps be solved most satisfactorily by a Lend-Lease arrangement with China to supply suitable Amphibious Labor Battalions of coolies armed with

212 *Ibid.,* Annex CHARLIE to Report of Operations of Commander Task Unit 81.2.3—Communications, pp. 1-2.

213 *Ibid.,* Annex DOG to Report of Operations of Commander Task Unit 81.2.3—Lessons Learned and Recommendations, pp. 1-2.

214 *Ibid.,* pp. 2-3.

215 *Ibid.,* pp. 3, 9.

gin poles, there are certain obstacles to be overcome before this solution could be applied.

One of Dierdorff's proposed means for resolving this problem was to simply recognize that unloading teams could not be expected to work round the clock without respite and perform their task efficiently. Thus, it should be realized that "after twenty-four to thirty-six hours of steady slogging through water and sand, dodging bombs and strafing" the shore crews would not be at their best. He advocated not only that the shore crews should be more adequately manned than before, but that a policy be adopted which would prohibit the operation of unloading details between 11:00 PM and dawn. He also urged that there be no division of command authority between the Army and Navy on the beach—the beachmasters should have complete command of everything occurring on the beach, his authority terminating only when the troops moved inland.

Transport Division Five, commanded by W.O. Bailey on board the USS *Charles Carroll*, had a very rough experience in the HUSKY operation. This Division, operating as Task Unit 85.2.2, left Oran on July 5, 1943. It arrived in its assigned transport area at 12:15 AM on July 10 and dropped anchor. The task unit was an hour behind schedule as a result of bad weather on the approach. While the heavy seas, which were caused by a northwest wind "of almost gale velocity," had diminished by the time the task unit had arrived off Sicily, the wind and sea were still heavy enough to make it very difficult to lower and load boats for two hours after their arrival. Bailey's task unit was to assault beaches GREEN-2 and YELLOW-2. [216]

Between 3:30 AM and 4:00 AM all units of the groups' Fire Support Group, including the USS *Philadelphia* and HMS *Abercrombie*, shelled GREEN-2 and YELLOW-2. The *Carroll*'s primary control vessel departed for the beach at 3:45 AM At about 4:00 AM parachute flares began to fall, first in the CENT area to the north, and then illuminating Bailey's transport area. At 4:40 AM enemy aircraft attacked the task unit in the face of heavy anti-aircraft fire. Several bombs landed near the *Carroll*, at distances from 600 to 900 yards. [217]

Control boats from the USS *Thomas Jefferson* got off course, causing waves to land not only on GREEN-2 and YELLOW-2, but also on the rocks between YELLOW-2 and an adjoining beach, BLUE-2. Some of the *Carroll*'s waves also landed near BLUE-2, although others landed on the proper beaches. At 6:00 AM the task unit began to move toward inshore anchorages with the *Thomas Jefferson* in the lead. At 6:15, however, the *Jefferson* and her sister ships came under heavy and accurate shellfire and "retired to the original Transport Area at full speed." The task unit was able to move to the inshore anchorage at 7:36 AM [218]

On July 10 unfavorable surf and beach conditions caused the stranding of many landing boats, causing unloading to be considerably slowed. Nevertheless, a large number of vehicles and most personnel were landed. At about 5:00 PM the task unit moved to inshore anchorages off Scoglitti, in order to unload on BLUE beach and RED-2 beach. However, unloading proceeded slowly after RED-2 was found unusable and BLUE beach was limited to the discharge of vehicles because of inadequate shore party to unload other cargo. [219]

The *Carroll* and her sister ships endured attacks by enemy aircraft late on July 10 and then again early on the morning of the following day, but without incident. At 10:00 AM on July 11 Bailey received an order to relocate his task unit so that it would be unloading on beaches BLUE, YELLOW and RED, as well as on YELLOW-2, all in the area of Scoglitti. Nevertheless, unloading continued to go slowly because of limited beach facilities and the fact that Bailey's unit could not get assistance from any shore parties. Only large landing craft could be used. During the afternoon enemy aircraft attacked the beach, but were driven off by anti-aircraft fire and Allied fighters. [220]

With the coming of darkness an intense struggle with the enemy began. Shortly before 8:00 PM the CENT area went on red alert. Some of the ships fired on high altitude Allied aircraft. About an hour later Bailey observed a tremendous explosion and fire at sea; at about the same time parachute flares illuminated the entire DIME area to Bailey's northwest, and he observed a large amount of anti-aircraft fire and some falling bombs. Then the CENT area was also illuminated by parachute flares. Bombs began to fall in and around the task unit, followed by more parachute flares.

From about 2240 up to 2300 both over land and sea the area in the immediate vicinity of

[216] Memorandum from W.O. Bailey, Commander Transport Division Five, to Commander Amphibious Force, U.S. Atlantic Fleet, dated July 17, 1943; Subject: Operation HUSKY, report of; USMC Collection, Box 117, File No. 24, pp. 1-3.

[217] *Ibid.*, p. 3.

[218] *Ibid.*, p. 4.

[219] *Ibid.*, p. 5.

[220] *Ibid.*

Scoglitti and our ships was a holocaust of low flying planes, anti-aircraft tracer fire, and shrapnel, with a great number of ships and shore batteries opening fire at low elevations and thereby endangering other ships in the area. It is doubtful whether one ship in this task unit escaped being hit by anti-aircraft fire several times. [221]

The worst was yet to come. At about 10:45 PM a large and unidentified aircraft, flying at low altitude to seaward, passed over the USS *Susan B. Anthony* and close aboard the *Procyon*. The two ships shot the plane out of the sky, and it crashed near the *Philadelphia*. Shortly, another similar plane also flying seaward "passed over the beach and was subjected to intense fire." The aircraft, which turned out to be a C-47, turned on its running lights and landed in the water. The *Carroll* rescued its crew. Bailey saw at least five other aircraft go down near the beach during the night. [222]

Bailey's task unit passed the next two days without incident, leaving Sicilian waters on July 13 and arriving in Oran three days later. The controversy began forthwith. The commander of the *Carroll* was sharply critical of the performance of the Control Vessel assigned to his ship. His wrath was particularly directed at the officer in command of the Control Vessel, who "seemed intelligent and eager to cooperate." Moreover, the *Carroll*'s Commanding Officer had placed aboard the Control Vessel his most experienced "ship to shore" officer, with the understanding that his advice would be followed by the Control Vessel's commander. These expectations were not met. First, the boat commander refused to anchor in the rendezvous area. This resulted in "continual confusion in the rendezvous circle by his backing and filling in an endeavor to keep station." Next, he was duly informed that the *Carroll* was anchored about eight hundred yards south of her assigned position, but nevertheless proceeded to the beach as though this condition did not exist, ignoring on the way further instructions to change course so as to get to the point of departure. His failure to follow orders contributed to the fact that the second, third and fourth waves landed on the rocks between YELLOW-2 and BLUE-2. [223]

Mishaps plagued the Control Vessel of the *Thom-*

*as Jefferson* as well. It took its proper station and anchored in the rendezvous area, receiving its proper course to the beach from the *Thomas Jefferson* in a timely fashion. The Control Vessel's path to the beach was carefully tracked by radar. However, at the same time the Control Vessel arrived at the line of departure, the *Thomas Jefferson* received a report that the first wave had landed ashore. It was then discovered that what was thought to have been the Control Vessel on the radar plot was in fact a destroyer. [224]

The contribution made by the task unit's Support Boats was also problematical. One Support Boat Division "could hardly be considered much support during the entire assault landing." Four of the boats in the Division either failed to show up at all or were so late in arriving as to be useless. Of the two remaining boats, one had inoperative rocket projectors while the other was "in a sinking condition." Therefore, this Division offered no fire support whatever. The second Support Boat Division, although not at full strength, "carried out the assignment and mission to the letter, maintaining patrol stations, screening the boat waves and delivering an effective barrage fire, which apparently caused the beach defense to lose any stomach they might of had for opposition." [225]

Bailey offered comprehensive comments concerning all aspects of the operation. In addition to calling for more time to be allowed for the approach to the transport area, to allow for bad weather and its consequences, he opined that Scout Boats were the "weakest link in our chain" and should be more purposefully designed and equipped. He commented further that "[F]ailure of this boat to properly indicate the desired beach may well end at some time to disaster to an operation." Such boats should be of such heavy construction that they could serve as salvage boats as well. Bailey particularly urged that beaches be selected that were suitable for both assault landing and unloading. He also stressed the obvious, learned from harsh experience, that it is "impractical and unsatisfactory to shift beaches after the operation has once started." Bailey also called for specially designed salvage craft, one assigned to each transport vessel. He praised the LSTs and LCTs, particularly the latter, and called for their expanded use. [226]

Bailey's staff also contributed comments on the operation. They also called for more time to be allotted for the approach to the transport area, since one of the effects of being under unrealistic time con-

[221]  *Ibid.*, pp. 5-6.
[222]  *Ibid.*, p. 6.
[223]  *Ibid.*, "Report on Part Played in the Action by Control Vessels, Scout Boats, and Support Boats," Annex A to Report of Commander Transport Division Five on Operation HUSKY, pp. A-1, A-2.

[224]  *Ibid.*, p. A-2.
[225]  *Ibid.*, p. A-3.
[226]  *Ibid.*, pp. B-1-B-4.

straints was to generate confusion and weaken the hitting power of the assault. The staff likewise implicitly criticized the effectiveness of the scout boats, calling for them to be especially designed and equipped for the task. Pointed criticism was also offered regarding control boats:

> Control Vessels must be especially trained in their duties and preferably should be an integral part of each transport division. It is not sufficient that they herd, lead and dispatch waves of boats but that they do it by leading them to the correct line of departure and send them to the correct beaches.

The staff also reported that "[F]rom the CENT operations it would appear that we have much to learn before we can successfully unload equipment and supplies over beaches after the assault." They also criticized inadequate preparation and equipment for salvage and traffic control, both of which directly contributed to rendering beaches congested and nearly unusable. The staff's most telling commentary, however, was also its most general one:

> We should revert to our original training systems; actually combat load troops and equipment. Move to the training area and unload troops and impedimenta over beaches. Simulate nothing. We are weak in beach discipline, traffic control and the unloading and handling of loaded boats on the beach. Of course, boats and equipment will be damaged, but it is infinitely better to learn to cope with those conditions on friendly shores than to try to cope with them under hostile attack. The next time we may not be facing an enemy who lacks stomach for a fight. [227]

Major General Troy H. Middleton, commanding officer of the U.S. 45th Infantry Division, provided a set of comments and recommendations on the HUSKY operation on July 31, 1943. One of his primary recommendations from the experience of his unit in Sicily was that it could have used a light tank company in lieu of one of the medium tank companies belonging to the medium tank battalion that had been attached to 45th Infantry Division. In fact, Middleton's division traded the 1st Infantry Division a medium tank company from one of the latter's light companies later in the operation. Middleton's main concern in this matter was the greater maneuverabil-

ity of the light tanks. He said that he considered tanks to be "an essential part of an infantry division," and said that their mere presence did much for the morale of infantry units. [228]

Middleton praised the addition of the 2d Chemical Battalion to his unit for the operation, while noting that their success was in spite of inadequate transport equipment. On the other hand, self propelled 105mm howitzers specially brought by the division from the U.S. did not particularly prove their worth. Middleton did not find it "essential" to use this weapon in place of medium artillery or to provide them as alternative weapons. [229]

Middleton found a Quartermaster Battalion attached to his division as labor troops to be sorely lacking in capability. He was more harsh still regarding the detail of a combat force, in this case the 40th Combat Engineers, to perform shore party work.

From the beginning this organization had a combat complex. The officers and men of the regiment were a "rabble," when they joined the Division at Camp Pickett, Virginia.

> While some improvement was noted, I still consider them a very poor organization and in general they performed mediocre service as Shore Party troops. Shore Party duty is labor duty and only first class labor troops should be assigned thereto. [230]

The General was critical of the logistics of the Sicily operation. For example, he pointed out that no combat unit should be loaded in the U.S. In the case of his own division, he noted that it embarked on May 28 and remained aboard ship until July 10, except for one week in North Africa. Another reason for not loading in the U.S. was its great distance from the theatre of action, which resulted in such anomalies as carrying the wrong equipment and clothing. Finally, Middleton concluded that amphibious training should occur near the theatre of operations, rather than in such places as Virginia, where the 45th Infantry Division had trained. [231]

Carl F. Robison commanded LCI(L) No. 1. His boat came under enemy fire at about 5:10 AM on July 10 near Graffi, from three emplacements with 24mm cannon and two other positions, one with a

---

[227] *Ibid.*, pp. C-1-C-4.

[228] Troy H. Middleton, Major General, U.S. Army Commanding, Report of 45th Division, HUSKY Operation, to Commander-in-Chief, United States Fleet, dated September 29, 1943, USMC Collection, Box 116, File No. 11, p. 1.

[229] *Ibid.*

[230] *Ibid.*, p. 2.

[231] *Ibid.*, pp. 2-3.

37mm and the other with a 75mm gun. Robison's controls and communications equipment were shot out, so that the boat approached the beach at low speed and essentially out of control. The ship swung around until its stern was to the beach, forcing the soldiers to disembark from the stern. Robison's boat stayed under fire until 6:45 AM. His number 1 gun crew fired off all of its 960 rounds at the enemy. Of Robison's three remaining guns, only crew no. 3 managed to fire 300 rounds. One of the remaining guns jammed on the first shot, while the other was silenced by enemy action. Three of his crew were killed and three more wounded.

In spite of the evident severity of his ship's contact with the enemy, Robison made the following very telling comments:

> The opposition encountered was not very determined, many of their guns were not knocked out and a large supply of ammunition was at hand. The guns on the bluff overlooking the beach were apparently abandoned at the first salvo by destroyers of our fire support group. The mobile units farther back also withdrew at this time...If the opposition had been a determined foe I do not believe troops could have been put ashore without first laying down a barrage and blasting the enemy out of their positions. [232]

Robison's colleague, Lieutenant H.G. Lippitt, was in command of USS LCI(L) Number 3. On July 5, 1943 his boat embarked 166 officers and men of company H, 2d Battalion, 7th Infantry Regiment of 3d Infantry Division in Tunisia. They arrived in the JOSS area (RED beach) on July 10. Lippitt's boat was in the first wave, and as they approached the area was illuminated by searchlights and flares. Lippitt's wave, however, was forced to circle for a period of time, waiting for the first wave of smaller boats to arrive. On their second approach Lippitt's wave hit the beach about twenty five feet from shore in a heavy surf and one and a half feet of water. The boats in Lippitt's wave had come under machine gun fire from both flanks. Like Robison, Lippitt had to use his engines to maintain the boat ashore. Both ramps were lost, and efforts to unload the troops by rubber boat and ladder failed. The troops were only disembarked after one of the ramps was located and placed back in working order. Lippitt's boat returned to Tunisia and made a second trip to Sicily, delivering another 130 men to the Licata area on July 12. [233]

The experience of Richard W. Caldwell, commanding USS LCI(L) Number 5, was a gruesome one. Number 5 took part in the assault on RED beach as part of the JOSS force. At 3:30 AM on July 10 the boat took aboard the commander of the 7th Infantry Regiment and his staff. Shortly after 4:00 AM Caldwell moved toward RED beach, encountering a substantial delay because the beach was not well marked. As the boat approached nearer the beach, it came under fire from anti-aircraft and machine guns, and Caldwell had to change course to avoid cannon fire. The beach was crowded with LCIs. At about 5:15 AM, under heavy shell fire, Caldwell's boat hit the beach about 150 feet from shore. Almost immediately Number 5 lost its starboard ramp in a collision with another LCI. The port ramp was then lost in the heavy surf. Efforts to substitute for the ramps with ladders and special lines failed utterly. The heavy surf, strong current and heavy equipment carried by the men made it impossible for them to get ashore, and those who tried foundered. Caldwell saw the corpses of soldiers, shot or drowned, floating in the surf. At 7:05 AM a round from what Caldwell described as an 88mm gun struck his ship and exploded inside one of the troop compartments, killing three soldiers instantly and seriously wounding several others. Number 5's anti-aircraft guns put the enemy weapon out of action. With the agreement of the regimental commander Caldwell then broached his boat ashore and the troops were able to disembark over the side. At about 8:00 AM Number 5 began taking on wounded. Caldwell and one of his sailors removed what was left of one soldier's arm and applied first aid. Caldwell and his boat stayed on the beach until about 3:00 PM, when it was pulled off. [234]

Lieutenant Willard W. Ayres commanded USS LCI(L) Number 9, designated as the wave leader of the first LCI(L) wave in the Gaffi Attack Group, part of the JOSS Attack Force. Ayres' boat had aboard the wave commander, Lieutenant Commander E.W. Wilson, and 138 men of the Headquarters Company, 2d Battalion, 7th Infantry Regiment. Ayres' wave was to follow two waves of assault troops on board LCVPs, whose job it was to destroy beach defenses. The men aboard the LCI(L)s were to land and move

[232] Action Report, Beach 73, From Carl F. Robison, Commanding Officer, USS LCI(L) No. 1, to Commander Red Attack Group, dated July 15, 1943, USMC Collection, Box 116, File No. 10.

[233] Action Report of the Invasion of Sicily, from H.G. Lippitt, Commanding Officer, USS LCI(L) No. 3, to Commander-in-Chief U.S. Fleet, dated July 16, 1943, USMC Collection, Box 116, File No. 10.

[234] Report of Action, Red Beach, JOSS Operation, July 10, 1943, from Richard W. Caldwell, Commanding Officer, USS LCI(L) No. 5, to Commander-in-Chief, U.S. Fleet, dated July 11, 1943, USMC Collection, Box 116, File No. 10.

inland immediately.

The first LCI(L) wave sortied from Sousse in North Africa. During its entire passage to Sicily it encountered a strong northwest wind and extremely heavy seas. This caused the LSTs in the Gaffi Attack Group to be an hour behind schedule. This, of course, delayed the entire operation of the Attack Group.

The LCI(L) first wave left for the beach at approximately 2:45 AM with Ayres in the lead of a V formation. The entire formation spent the next hour and a half going back and forth, to and from the beach, because of uncertainty as to whether the assault boats had gone to the beach. Ayres stopped the formation about 800 yards from the shore and took soundings. There was no activity on the beach until 4:40 AM when the enemy opened fire with 20 mm cannon and machine guns. Ayres advanced toward the beach and dropped anchor 150 yards from shore. Ayres lowered the ramps and all troops were disembarked by 5:00 AM, in the face of continuous machine gun and small arms fire. Ayres' boat withheld its fire on order from Commander Wilson, because the enemy positions could not be identified. One of Ayres' crewmen was killed, and two soldiers wounded. Ayres made an unsuccessful attempt to rescue LCI(L) Number 1 during its "magnificent battle" with the enemy gun emplacements. Ayres and his boat returned to North Africa after their failed rescue attempt. [235]

USS LCI(L) Number 10 acted as the headquarters ship for the Gaffi Attack Group and flagship for the task group commander, Task Group 86.2. It carried the commanders and staffs of both the 7th Regimental Combat Team and the Gaffi Attack Group. Its commander was W.A. Drisler, Jr. Number 10's trip to the war zone was eventful in itself. The ship left Bizerte after embarking its troops during an air raid, bound for the staging area at Sousse. From there it proceeded to Sicilian waters "through heavy chop," arriving with half of the embarked troops in a state of seasickness. During the passage the communications officer of the 7th Regimental Combat Team was swept overboard, but miraculously recovered uninjured by another LCI.

Early on the morning of July 10, Drisler's boat transferred the staff of 7th Regimental Combat Team to LCI(L) Number 5. For the next hour and a half, the ship was under continuous air attack, but without

incident. The rest of the day was spent driving off more enemy air attacks and trying unsuccessfully to rescue stranded LCIs. The next day was also heavy with anti-aircraft action. Drisler's ship claimed to have downed at least one Stuka dive bomber. [236]

USS LCI(L) Number 209 was in the second LCI wave landing on beach 73, RED beach, as part of the Gaffi Attack Group. The boat carried 130 officers and men of Company L, 2d Battalion, 7th Infantry Regiment, and was commanded by Lieutenant Kenneth E. Leake. Number 209 beached at 5:00 AM, approximately ten yards from the shore and 300 yards from LCI(L) Number 1. The boat was under fire from enemy machine guns, mortars and cannon, all directed from a steep cliff overlooking the beach. Leake's boat refrained from returning fire for a time, out of fear of endangering American troops. The boat finally opened up with its no. 1 20mm cannon after it became apparent that the enemy positions had to be reduced if the troops were to get ashore without heavy casualties.

Leake reported that the gun's first burst "disintegrated" an enemy soldier who was unsuccessfully throwing hand grenades at the boat from a distance of 25 yards. The gun also eliminated two machine gun nests and several snipers. As a result of this covering fire the infantry were able to disembark successfully, only one of their number being mortally wounded between boat and shore. Leake's craft escaped serious damage, and only one of its crew was slightly wounded. [237]

Colonel H.E. Smyser, USA, served as logistics representative on the staff of Commander Amphibious Force, United States Atlantic Fleet, during the HUSKY operation. He attended the invasion and follow-on operations in Sicily in that capacity, and provided a written report of his observations, complete with extensive photographs, on August 9, 1943. [238]

Discussing the experience of the 45th Infantry Division, which he noted obtained its final objective of the first phase of the operation on D+5, Smyser pointed out that "[D]irect hits by naval gunfire on

[235] Action Report of Landing on Punta Di Gaffi (Red) Beach, Sicily, JOSS Attack Force, July 10, 1943, from Willard W. Ayres, Commanding Officer, USS LCI(L) No. 9, to Commander-in-Chief, United States Fleet, dated July 25, 1943, USMC Collection, Box 116, File No. 10.

[236] Report of Operations, Sicilian Invasion, from W.A. Drisler, Jr., Commanding Officer, USS LCI(L) No. 10 to Commander, LCI(L) Flotilla II, dated July 24, 1943, USMC Collection, Box 116, File No. 10.

[237] Action Report from Kenneth E. Leake, Commanding Officer, USS LCI(L) No. 209 to Commander, LCI(L) Flotilla Two, dated July 12, 1943, USMC Collection, Box 116, File No. 10.

[238] Memorandum to Commander Amphibious Force, United States Atlantic Fleet, Subject: Report on Operation HUSKY covering the period D—D+7 days, by Colonel H.E. Smyser, USA, dated August 9, 1943, USMC Collection, Box 117, File No. 22.

gun emplacements and concrete pillboxes contributed greatly to the rapid advance of the 45th Division inland." Smyser attributed the fact that the "initial landings were made practically without opposition" to the effect of this naval preparatory fire. [239]

Smyser's report noted that initially the landing beaches were designated RED, GREEN, YELLOW, GREEN-2, YELLOW-2 and BLUE-2. On D-Day, however, Smyser and others from 45th Infantry Division G-4 arrived in Scoglitti and conducted a beach survey. It was then decided to abandon RED, GREEN and YELLOW as of noon on D+1 and to establish six new beaches, namely RED, GREEN and YELLOW north of Scoglitti, RED-2 and GREEN-2 in the town of Scoglitti and YELLOW-2 south of Scoglitti. On the afternoon of D+1 it was decided to abandon the three remaining original beaches and to concentrate on the beaches in the Scoglitti area. The new beaches were organized and dedicated for certain purposes (e.g., RED and GREEN- ammunition; YELLOW-rations) in anticipation of the arrival of a major supply convoy on D+4. [240]

In the area of the 45th Infantry Division Smyser found the organization of the beaches to be generally inadequate. Debarkation points were poorly marked and coxswains paid little attention to the markings that existed. Beach parties did not check the arrival of supplies. Beach exit roads were inadequately improved, even though adequate equipment for this purpose was available. Senior commanders had trouble controlling shore parties because of inadequate communication on and between beaches. The most serious problem was that supplies piled up on the beaches and blocked exits. This problem was difficult to resolve even though there was ample labor available for unloading, including hundreds of Italian prisoners. [241]

Smyser found the performance of beach parties in Sicily to be a vast improvement over beach party operation in TORCH. Some problems remained. Among these were the obvious ones pointed out by many others---the need for beachmasters, for example, to have appropriate rank. Smyser recommended the ranks of Lt. Commander and Commander for regimental and divisional beachmasters respectively. The mundane as well came in for scrutiny---Smyser observed that the beach parties lacked waterproof covers for their weapons, rendering many arms unserviceable. Most importantly, beach parties should be armed with rifles, as opposed to the pistols with which they had been issued. This problem had almost

become of critical importance at Gela and on the left flank of the 45th Infantry Division, where fortunately enemy counterattacks did not penetrate to the beach. [242]

Smyser's comments on the operation and suitability of the various landing craft used in Sicily are noteworthy. He classed together the LST, LCI(L), LCT and LCM, finding all of them suitable, but singling out the LST as "outstanding in performance and usefulness." On the other hand, the LCVP was found to be "disappointing" in both operation and suitability, its primary drawback being its undependability. Smyser noted that several hours after landing, an average of about 70 of these vessels were constantly out of action on RED and GREEN beaches north of Scoglitti. Most impressive to Smyser were the new DUKWS, which demonstrated to him a superior ability for unloading any type of ship. For Smyser, the DUKW "definitely is the best answer for the movement of supplies from ships into organized beach dumps." [243]

Preparations for HUSKY had included provision for heavy casualties. In the event, more than sufficient facilities, equipment and trained personnel were on hand for the evacuation of those wounded during the landing phase. As Smyser noted, "[P]robably never before in modern warfare were soldiers so promptly evacuated from the battlefield or given such excellent care as on OPERATION HUSKY." [244]

Smyser was particularly gratified by the success of palletized loading of supplies . This was the first occasion on which this system was utilized, and in Smyser's view it greatly facilitated both loading and unloading, and more importantly, movement from shore to supply dumps farther inland. According to Smyser, however, during his entire eight day stay on the island he was constantly plagued by snipers shooting at him from nearby fields. [245]

Captain John H. Leppert, USN, commanded Task Group 81.4. On D-4, Captain Leppert arrived at Sousse with the LCI(L)s of DIME, CENT and KOOL, anchoring out at dark. Because of the very large number of landing craft involved, and attendant concerns about concentrating so many ships in the harbor, over the next two days Leppert's unit went through a complicated disembarking and re-embarking procedure until all ships were loaded and anchored away from the berths. In all, Leppert had 52 ships under his command. [246]

[239]  *Ibid.*, p. 2.
[240]  *Ibid.*, pp. 4-5.
[241]  *Ibid.*, p. 5.

[242]  *Ibid.*, pp. 7-8.
[243]  *Ibid.*, p. 8.
[244]  *Ibid.*, p. 10.
[245]  *Ibid.*, pp. 11-12.
[246]  Memorandum by Captain John H. Leppert, USN, Com-

Just before midnight on July 8, 1943 Task Group 81.4 got underway from Sousse, Leppert having first admonished his commanding officers that "if any ship became high and dry it was still a fighting unit as long as it had guns and was above the surface of the water." At dawn on July 9 the seas increased, so that eventually Leppert's LCI(L) column had to increase its speed to maximum in order to close with the transport column. Upon closing with the USS *Dickman*, his assigned transport, Leppert reverted to command of the three ships in his LCI(L) division one, LCI(L)s 17, 188 and 189. By continuing to press these vessels at maximum speed, which made the soldiers aboard very sick, Leppert managed to keep up with the *Dickman*, despite "considerable pounding" to his own ships.[247]

On the first attempt, LCI (L) Number 189 was the only one of Leppert's ships to successfully beach. The other two boats became hung up on sand bars and had to be retracted and re-beached. In addition to troops, Leppert's boats carried supply carts weighing up to 400 lbs., and these caused a good deal of trouble during unloading. In spite of these difficulties, unloading was successfully accomplished, and during the afternoon of July 10 Leppert received orders to depart for Tunis with 17 LCI(L)s. Leppert and 14 LCI(L)s returned to Sicily on July 13 and delivered more troops to the DIME and CENT beaches without incident.[248]

Among the boats under Leppert's command was LCI(L) Number 17, H.G. Stender commanding. Stender's boat was Leppert's flagship, and in addition to the Task Group commander and his staff, carried 200 men of Company A, 83d Chemical Battalion, Major William S. Hutchinson, Jr. in command. Number 17 also carried 12 two-wheeled carts bearing 4.2 in. mortars, 12 additional carts filled with mortar rounds, and 36 additional boxes of mortar ammunition. Stender and his boat arrived in the DIME area at 9:30 PM on July 9. At 11:30 PM Stender observed the effects of the U.S. glider and paratroop attack near Gela, and fifteen minutes later saw U.S. transport aircraft pass overhead on their way to Africa without incident. At 2:30 AM on July 10 Number 17 fell in behind the first wave of smaller craft headed for the beach, followed by LCI(L)s Numbers 188 and 189.

After some considerable delay Number 17 dropped anchor about 200 yards from the beach and 100 yards to the east of the pier at Gela. However, it struck a sand bar about 15 yards from the beach and eventually a strong current broached the boat parallel to the beach. Only with the aid of two LCVPs could Stender's boat be freed, and not until almost 7:00 AM During its stranding on the sand bar Number 17 became the target of enemy gunfire. Starting at about 5:15 AM three batteries on Cape Soprano began firing. Stender believed these guns to be German 88mm cannon, and 25 of their shells landed in the water near his boat over the space of an hour and a quarter. Two rounds struck the ship, the first a glancing blow and the second a more serious hit that exploded inside the boatswain's locker. This shell did considerable damage but caused no casualties.

Although Stender's boat managed to disembark all of its troops while stuck on the sandbar, it could not disgorge its cargo because of the depth of the water. It required another landing on GREEN beach to disembark the carts and other cargo. After another trip to the beach with rations and ammunition, Number 17 returned to Tunis with Captain Leppert's convoy of LCI(L)s. There the boat was repaired and refueled, and on July 13 it embarked another 180 soldiers, including Brigadier General Norman D. Cota and elements of the 17th Field Artillery, 809th Engineers and 15th Evacuation Hospital. Stender delivered these troops to GREEN beach near Gela on July 14 without incident. Number 17 returned to Tunis on July 15 for the final time, its crew having suffered no casualties.[249]

LCI(L) Number 188 got underway from Sousse shortly before midnight on July 8, 1943. By morning the wind was from the north, causing the boat to roll considerably, resulting in "general seasickness" among the embarked troops. Nevertheless, the boat reached the transport area off Sicily very early on July 10, and went into the beach at 3:50 AM Like Number 17, however, the ship found itself on a sand bar 17 feet from the beach, in about eight feet of water. Despite repeated efforts to retract, the boat remained stuck fast.

Number 188 made the mistake of lowering both of her ramps on grounding, nearly losing both of them. It was only through strenuous efforts by the crew that all of the ship's cargo was eventually unloaded. This process consumed more than three hours, during which time the boat was twice hit by enemy artillery shells, resulting in injuries to one crewman and four soldiers. The boat's commander

mander Task Group 81.4 to Commander Task Force 81, Subject: Operations—HUSKY; report of, dated July 26, 1943, USMC Collection, Box 117, File No. 17, p. 1.

[247] *Ibid.*, p. 2.

[248] *Ibid.*, pp. 2-3.

[249] *Ibid.*, Enclosure A, Memorandum from H.G. Stender, Commanding Officer, USS LCI(L) No. 17, to Commander Task Group 81.4, Subject: Action in HUSKY Operations, Report of, dated July 18, 1943, pp. 1-4.

had a generally negative impression of his human cargo.

The Army proved more of a hindrance than a help in the whole operation. They lay on the deck in the passageways forcing our men to walk on weather decks to move from Bow to Stern. They had no organization in handling carts and they caused great delay by refusing to obey the orders of my officers in trying to establish some order out of the chaos. When they did unload the mortar carts they moved much too slowly and they were loathe to leave when carts were off. A great deal of their equipment was left behind including packs, signal flags and ammunition. [250]

The third boat in Leppert's small flotilla was USS LCI(L) Number 189, commanded by Lt. (jg) Edward S. Dulcan. Like its sisters, Number 189 got underway from Sousse near midnight on July 8, and encountered heavy seas the following morning. Although the heavy weather caused some sickness among the troops aboard, Dulcan thought the men were less affected than they had been in the pre-invasion rehearsals. On the evening of July 9 the vessel made contact with the transports, which were an hour behind schedule and therefore making greater speed than planned in order to make up the lost time. In order to keep up with the transports, Dulcan had to force his craft to maintain very high speed.

Although it encountered some machine gun and cannon fire, by 4:00 am. Number 189 was grounded about 20 yards off the beach in about four feet of water. Dulcan then gave the order to disembark. This occurred at a "snail's pace." This was due partially to the fact that the starboard ramp quickly became inoperative, and remained so in spite of the crew's efforts to repair it. This required all the troops to debark on the port ramp, and this was completed at 5:10 AM, when Dulcan retracted and headed out to sea. He and his ship made two more successful runs to the beach without incident. [251]

There were another sixteen boats under Leppert's command in Sicily. It is indicative of the state of the Axis defenses on the island that virtually none of them suffered casualties to either their crews or their embarked troops. Indeed, many of their commanding officers expressly recounted how they encountered no resistance whatever. Of those boats which actually fired their weapons, many did so at aircraft that were safely out of range.

J. B. Freese, Commander Task Unit 86.1221, had 25 LCTs under his command, all of which landed on YELLOW beach on July 10. All were fully loaded with troops and equipment. All successfully delivered their cargo and personnel without loss. [252]

Robert L. Coleman commanded USS LST Number 311, a part of LST Group One. His boat sailed from Tunis as part of a convoy of LSTs in the JOSS and CENT attack forces. Off Gozo Light the convoy divided, Number 311 joining the DIME force. On July 10 it unloaded its cargo without incident. On the evening of that day, it received a pontoon causeway from the USS *Hopi* and immediately set about rigging it out on RED beach. With the causeway nearly ready for use, Coleman's boat and two others, 370 and 312, came under attack by three Me 109Fs. Two bombs landed near 312 and one near 311, the latter breaking the lashings between the pontoons and causing half of it to broach on the beach. This scattered the crew, and rigging commenced again only after some delay.

At 6:30 PM the three boats were joined by USS LST Number 313, and five minutes later the lot of them came under attack by three Me 109Fs. Number 313 suffered a direct hit from a bomb, which detonated the ammunition on board and set fire to gasoline and vehicles. Needless to say, the explosion killed those in the immediate vicinity. Those who survived began abandoning ship from the bow and stern, some swimming for shore. Coleman's ship turned its hoses on Number 313, but his craft was not close enough for the water to reach the fire. One of the attacking aircraft crashed, a victim of anti-aircraft fire. Coleman was forced to retract, "inasmuch as the explosions and heat from the wreck were unbearable." A few minutes later Coleman maneuvered the bow of his ship against the stern of Number 313 and was able to remove about 81 men. Others were rescued from the water by man lines. During the entire rescue operation Coleman's boat was showered with debris and shrapnel from the Number 313's cargo. After finally retracting, Coleman delivered 25 badly wounded men to a hospital ship. Coleman's boat anchored for the night in the transport area.

[250] *Ibid.,* Enclosure B, Memorandum from Commanding Officer, USS LCI(L) 188 to Commander Flotilla One, Subject Action Report, dated July 18, 1943, pp. 1-2.

[251] *Ibid.,* Enclosure C, Memorandum from Lt. (jg) Edward S. Dulcan, Commanding Officer, USS LCI(L) No. 189 to Commander, Flotilla One, Subject: Action Report, dated July 18, 1943, pp. 1-3.

[252] Memorandum from J.B. Freese, Commander Task Unit 86.1221 to Commander-in-Chief, United States Fleet, dated 7 August 1943, Subject: Invasion of Sicily on 10 July 1943, Action and Operations Report On, USMC Collection, Box 116, File No. 14.

On July 11 activity began at just prior to 7:00 am, when enemy bombers attacked the transport area, scoring a hit on the USS *Barnett*. An hour later Coleman's boat began disembarking men and cargo, enlisting the aid of another LST to help unload. Starting at about noon, Number 311 and her sisters came under fairly constant enemy air attacks for a period lasting over ten hours. During this time Coleman's crew repeatedly engaged the enemy aircraft, for the most part ineffectively, although one German aircraft was reported as a probable kill. Late in the afternoon, during one of these attacks, Coleman observed that two "Liberty" ships were hit by bombs. The first exploded and sank, while the second caught fire and burned fiercely. Coleman's boat, however, escaped damage, and his crew were uninjured.

Coleman's Executive Officer was James T. Smith, who authored his own report of the action at Sicily. His observations corroborate those of his commanding officer. His comments concerning the state of the defenses, however, merit special attention.

The defenders were evidently taken by surprise because there seemed to be very little resistance in the early hours of the invasion. In my opinion, they were not quite able to comprehend just what was going on. The attacking naval warships were very efficient in silencing and extinguishing the coastal defense batteries and searchlights of the enemy. At 1100 the first enemy resistance became apparent to us as the C.D. batteries began to shell the LSTs 312, 338 and 344 beached on RED No. 2 sector of Beach No. 67. There didn't seem to be any enemy bombers in the vicinity although there were a few fighters now and then. [253]

USS LST Number 381, commanded by E.F. Marcellus, formed part of Task Unit 86.1216 landing on RED 2. It unloaded troops and equipment on July 10, in spite of intense enemy air activity. The following day it resumed this activity, finally unloading all its cargo by about 3:00 PM From that time on until midnight the boat came under consistent air and artillery attack, but without suffering damage. The persistent enemy air attacks had one unintended result, namely the predisposition of Navy gunners to fire at any aircraft, frequently before identifying them. Marcellus observed this first hand when at about 11:00 PM he saw an unidentified aircraft crash land in the water nearby. Marcellus sent out an LCVP to look for survivors. The unidentified aircraft, which had been shot down by Navy gunfire, turned out to be a U.S. Army transport plane from the 62d Troop Carrier Squadron, 314th Troop Carrier Wing. The LCVP was able to rescue only two survivors, 1st Lt. Donald A. Broadus and 2d Lt. Michael B. Webb. [254]

Colonel Eugene M. Caffey commanded 1st Engineer Special Brigade, which provided three Engineer Shore Groups for the landings, each with one of three reinforced infantry regiments, landing at Licata, Gela and Scoglitti. The Brigade numbered about 20,000 men, and had two principal responsibilities, namely (1) the landing of troops, equipment and supplies and the establishment of beach dumps; and (2) the execution of all supply plans of the Seventh Army. [255]

There was little difficulty for the Brigade in carrying out unloading operations as planned, because of "ideal weather... an almost total lack of enemy interference after D+1, and ...the use of the small ports of Licata and Empedocle." In fulfilling its obligations as the first step in supplying the Seventh Army, the Brigade relied upon the Sicilian railroads, which had been only slightly damaged and were being put back in operation as early as D+1, and "were the decisive factor in the rapid pushing forward of the supply lines because there were simply not half enough supply vehicles to have carried the tonnage which the rapid advance demanded." [256]

Like many others, Caffey was very pleased with the DUKWS, finding that "their performance was up to advance expectations." On the subjects of "basic soldiering" and discipline in the Brigade, however, Caffey was less sanguine.

The operation showed the need for more and better instruction of the individual officer and soldier. They need detailed instruction in clean and orderly living in the field; how to get along with little and make that little do; how to take care of arms, equipment, and clothing and the necessity for doing so; their personal responsibility for government prop-

---

[253] Memorandum from Robert L. Coleman, Commanding Officer, USS LST 311, to Commander-in-Chief, U.S. Fleet, dated 27 July 1943, Subject: Action Report; Memorandum from James T. Smith, Executive Officer, USS LST 311 to the Commanding Officer, dated 27 July 1943, Subject: Action Report, USMC Collection, Box 117, File No. 30.

[254] Memorandum from E.F. Marcellus, Commanding Officer, USS LST Number 381 to the Commander-in-Chief, dated August 10, 1943, Subject: Action Report for Period 10-12 July, 1943, USMC Collection, Box 117, File No. 31.

[255] Colonel Eugene M. Caffey, Commanding Officer, 1st Engineer Special Brigade, "Shore Engineers in Sicily," dated 11 August 1943, USMC Collection, Box 117, File No. 16, p. 1.

[256] *Ibid.*

erty of all sorts. They must be taught and required to perform their individual duties. They need the alertness that comes from physical fitness and insistence on military courtesy and the smart performance of all duties. They need commanders of all grades who know what to do, how to teach others, and who are possessed of the physical strength to work all day and all night and the determination and the moral courage to exact from their subordinates a full performance of all their duties under all circumstances...

Instant and instinctive obedience has got to be taught to all ranks. Too much time is wasted in argument, discussion, and coaxing. It was found that commanders of all grades in the Brigade were reluctant, for one reason or another to take summary and certain action against the recalcitrant, the laggard, and the neglectful and shiftless. Either they were lazy, ignorant, or lacking in the necessary force of character or, based on past experience, they felt that they would not be supported or would be adversely criticized. The greatest need shown in this operation was the need of discipline on the part of individuals and control on the part of commanders. [257]

## THE POST-LANDING BATTLE IN BRIEF

While the Seventh Army encountered heavy weather and generally stiffer resistance, the degree of resistance varied from beach to beach. The landings at Scoglitti were virtually unopposed, and the beachhead was established ahead of schedule. The 1st Infantry Division encountered heavy opposition at some beaches and very little at others. 3rd Infantry Division met opposition only sporadically. [258]

In less than two days, 15th Army Group landed a total of about 80,000 men, 7,000 vehicles, 300 tanks and 900 guns, along with sufficient supplies to maintain all of these men and their equipment. As to the latter, for the first time the Allies made use of the amphibious DUKW, a vehicle which, according to Eisenhower, "more than any other technical factor, solved the problem of large-scale maintenance over the beaches." The work of the DUKWs was augmented almost immediately by the capture of several small ports. The Allies seized and reopened Licata on D-Day; they also took possession of Syracuse on that day, and by D+3 that port was receiving the ships of the D+3 convoy and their 16,000 troops, who dis-

charged in less than 4 hours. The Allies also took the port of Augusta on D+3. [259]

The Allies had expected to lose up to 300 of the 2000 vessels employed in the initial assault. In the event, in the British zone only 3 transports and a hospital ship ("fully illuminated") were sunk, while in the American sector 2 destroyers, 2 submarine chasers and 6 landing craft were sunk, and 20 additional landing craft were damaged. Such minimal losses as were suffered resulted from the fact that the Allies enjoyed overwhelming air superiority. Enemy air activity was limited and quickly repulsed. The enemy attacked the American ships 89 times in the first three days of the assault. Allied aircraft drove off 26 of these attacks before they reached their targets, and successfully engaged most of the remaining attacks over the Allied ships. [260]

In the first week of operations, the Seventh Army engaged both *Panzer-Division "Hermann Göring"* and *15. Panzer-Grenadier-Division,* including most of their tanks. These German forces launched four counterattacks before July 16, of which by far the most significant was that which occurred on July 11. On that day, German tanks penetrated to within 1000 yards of the 1st Infantry Division beachhead at Gela, and were driven off by a "devastating combination of rocket guns, anti-tank grenades, tanks, artillery, and naval gunfire, which knocked out between 10 and 16 of the 40-50 attacking tanks." The Germans began to withdraw after the failure of these counterattacks, successively disengaging from the Seventh Army front between July 17 and July 20, and moving into positions opposite the Eighth Army. [261]

Once the Allied armies were well established ashore, Eisenhower relinquished responsibility for direction of the campaign to 15th Army Group commander General Alexander and his subordinates, Patton and Montgomery. This was consistent with orders issued by Admiral Hewitt, commanding Western Naval Task force. Hewitt operated under so-called "joint agreements of the U.S. Army and Navy," under which in amphibious operations the naval commander commanded until the commanding general of the land forces had established his command post ashore. This latter step was regarded as taken when all of the assault forces had landed and established a beachhead of 10,000 yards in depth, so that the supply system of the landing force was operating in a normal manner. Hewitt's experience in HUSKY suggested to him that Army notions of amphibious operations had not kept pace with those of the Navy,

---

[257]   *Ibid.,* p. 8.

[258]   Eisenhower Dispatch, p. 26.

[259]   *Ibid.*

[260]   *Ibid.*

[261]   *Ibid.*

particularly with regard to the question of command and responsibility in such operations. Indicative of this was the fact that plans issued by Army commanders had set forth directives governing the disposition and use of naval craft, including firing and target schedules for vessels in Hewitt's task force. These misconceptions, according to Hewitt, stemmed from the fact that Army officers believed that they were in a position to exercise extensive authority while afloat, a circumstance which he attributed at least in part to the fact that the term "Headquarters Ship," in place of the proper term "Flagship," had come into Army parlance, particularly when referring to the vessel on which the commanding general of the landing force was embarked. The plan that these forces were intended to follow called for an advance up the east coast of the island by Eighth Army to the port of Messina, the ground campaign's major objective. During this advance, the Seventh Army was to protect Licata, Ponte Olivo, Biscari and Comiso, and to guard Eighth Army's left flank against enemy attack. Eighth Army, then, was to attack through Catania and Gerbini, while Seventh Army merely broadened its beachhead. As early as D+9, however, these plans were fundamentally reversed. The Germans concentrated their forces against the British and held them up in the Catania area, while Seventh Army moved "largely against Italians" northwest toward Palermo to cut the island in two. [262]

The Germans halted the advance of the Eighth Army at Catania on July 20, holding the British in position there until August 4. The principal German units engaged included the *Panzer-Division "Hermann Göring"* and *15. Panzer-Grenadier-Division,* as well as two regiments from *1. Fallschirm-Jaeger Division.* Here the enemy enjoyed the benefits of difficult terrain, the plain being criss-crossed by canals, drainage ditches and rivers, and German observers being well placed on the foothills of Mount Etna. Under these conditions the enemy were able to repeatedly pound the Eighth Army as it attempted to move forward from its bridgehead over the Dittaino River and into the plain of Catania. In order to bring maximum weight against the German forces, who were bitterly contesting every foot of ground, and to exploit the evident demoralization and weakness of the Italians, Alexander decided to make Palermo the main axis of supply for Seventh Army, and to move that force into line with Eighth Army for a breakthrough to Messina. Thus Seventh Army was to push through Palermo to the north coast of the island, and then to push toward Messina along two axes, the coastal road

and the road Petralia-Nicosia-Troina-Cesaro, which had formerly been designated as the Eighth Army's northern axis of advance. [263]

Following extremely fast advances over open country, 3rd Infantry Division and 2nd Armored Division met at Palermo on July 22 and encountered little resistance. The city surrendered at 10:00 PM. Next day Alexander issued an order directing Seventh Army to maintain strong pressure on the enemy's northern flank, moving eastward along the aforementioned twin axes, and leaving only minimal forces in western Sicily. The Seventh Army was to begin its drive on August 1. Alexander directed that supply bases were to be shifted to Palermo without delay. Patton placed all non-divisional artillery of Seventh Army under the command of II Corps, and moved 3rd Infantry Division and 9th Infantry Division into the sector of II Corps. The air forces were directed to bomb enemy communication and transportation systems in the northeast corner of the island. Naval Task Force 88, including 2 cruisers and 4-6 destroyers, was to operate along the island's north coast along Highway 133 to support Seventh Army with naval gunfire as needed, and to land advanced ground units when possible. Royal Navy ships were detailed to assist Eighth Army along the east coast in the same way. [264]

While Eighth Army enjoyed the benefit of supply lines coming from Augusta and Syracuse, both of which ports were in fair working order, the condition of Palermo was less favorable. Port capacity had been reduced to about 30% by the Allied bombing campaign, which had resulted in 44 vessels of all types having been sunk in the docks and the channels. Although 12 ships were able to disgorge the 9th Infantry Division there on August 1, it took another 30 days to raise the capacity of the harbor to 60% of its former level. Seventh Army was thus receiving supplies from both the west at Palermo and the south from Gela and Licata, and on August 3 a beach was opened at San Stefano, and this was used to supply the Army's advance for the next ten days. Following the Army's advance, new beaches were opened for supply, and these allowed the quick advance to continue in spite of the loss of road and rail facilities through bombing and enemy demolition. [265]

On July 28 Admiral Hewitt created Task Force 88 for the purpose of supporting the advance of Seventh Army by naval gunfire and effecting advance landings of military units. The force comprised three cruisers, fourteen destroyers and numerous smaller

---

[262] *Ibid.,* p. 27.

[263] *Ibid.,* p. 28.
[264] *Ibid.,* p. 29.
[265] *Ibid.,* p. 30.

vessels. After the capture of Palermo on July 22, 45th Infantry Division moved eastward along the northern coast toward Messina, reaching Cefalu on July 24. The advance continued to the road junction north of San Mauro on July 26, along Highway 113 to San Mauro on the following day, thence to a position four miles east of the Tusa River on July 29. Some units moved south to Mistretta, while others moved to the enemy flank near San Stefano. The next day the advancing Seventh Army met strong resistance from *Panzer-Grenadier-Regiment 71.* of *29. Panzer-Grenadier-Division.* The destroyer *Rowan* supported the troops. On July 31 the 45th Infantry Division took San Stefano. Using its own spotter plane, the cruiser *Philadelphia* bombarded San Stefano while being engaged by a 6 inch shore battery. The 3rd Infantry Division replaced the 45th Infantry Division on the left flank of Seventh Army, and advanced four miles east of San Stefano on August 1. On the night of August 2-3 the *Philadelphia, Rowan* and *Knight* laid down heavy fire on the coastal highway and on an enemy strongpoint near San Agata. On August 3, the *Philadelphia, Savannah, Gherardi* and *Rhind* shelled the same area, enabling 3rd Infantry Division to reach a position within two miles of the Furiano River.[266]

On August 4 Hewitt's forces observed a large concentration of enemy artillery on the coastal road. That morning the 15th Infantry Regiment encountered heavy resistance as it made an unsuccessful attack across the river under cover of naval gunfire. The regiment then moved up the valley about two miles in search of a more favorable route across the river. Later that day, as the 1st Infantry Division attack on Troina gained momentum, Hewitt's task force brought the 7th Regimental Combat Team and attached artillery in by sea in landing craft to the area behind the 15th Regimental Combat Team, about one mile west of the Furiano River and two miles west of San Fratello, in preparation for an attack on San Fratello Ridge. At the same time, the cruiser *Savannah* laid down heavy shellfire on numerous targets, including San Agata, Cape Orlando and highway 113, as well as bridges and defiles in the area. The shore battery at Cape Orlando returned the fire.[267]

During the night of August 4-5, the destroyers *Gherardi* and *Rhind* placed a bombardment on enemy positions near San Agata. On the following day, the 3rd Infantry Division continued its attack toward San Agata with the 30th Regimental Combat Team attacking San Fratello ridge from the southwest, while

the cruiser *Savannah* and destroyers *Rowan* and *Trippe* took under fire enemy positions between San Agata and Cape Orlando. The shore batteries near the latter point returned the fire. The next day the *Savannah* and *Rowan* bombarded enemy positions ahead of U.S. forces, who made an unsuccessful attempt to gain a foothold across the Fruiano. On August 7 the American ground forces encountered strong enemy resistance near the coast, in the form of a counterattack north of San Fratello. The cruisers *Savannah* and *Philadelphia* laid down heavy fire between San Agata and Cape Orlando on enemy concentrations.[268]

Early in the morning of August 8 Hewitt's task force made an amphibious landing in the rear of the enemy. The units landed consisted of one battalion of infantry, one tank platoon and two batteries of field artillery, and debarked near Terranova, six miles west of Cape Orlando. The cruisers *Philadelphia* and *Savannah* and the destroyers *Wainwright, Rhind, Rowan* and *Trippe* supported these units. The landing broke enemy resistance in San Fratello; 3rd Infantry Division occupied Mount Fratello and the towns of San Fratello and San Agata. On August 11 the task force made another amphibious landing in the enemy's rear, two miles east of Cape Orlando. On this occasion the force consisted of one infantry battalion, reinforced with armored artillery and tanks. The cruisers *Philadelphia* and *Boise* and the destroyers *Rowan, Rhind* and *Trippe* supported this landing. The enemy met the landing with artillery emplacements and 20mm guns in pillboxes on the beach; naval gunfire neutralized these positions. In addition, the *Philadelphia* broke up a German counterattack which threatened the forces that had just landed.[269]

On August 12 the 3rd Infantry Division moved into Cape Orlando. Under cover of gunfire from the cruiser *Boise*, 30th Regimental Combat Team moved down the coast road and took Brolo and Ficarra. That night, the destroyers *Benson* and *Plunkett* bombarded the coast road where enemy forces were withdrawing. The next day 3rd Infantry Division continued to advance toward Patti. The advance past Cape Calava, four miles northwest of Patti, was impeded by a large crater blown in the road at the eastern end of the Calava tunnel where the road had been carved from sold rock. The troops bypassed this roadblock by embarking in LCTs with their artillery and vehicles and being ferried around the cape to a point to the east of the road block.[270]

Early on the morning of August 16 Hewitt's task

---

[266]  Hewitt Report, p. 73.
[267]  *Ibid.*

[268]  *Ibid.*
[269]  *Ibid.,* p. 74.
[270]  *Ibid.*

force made another amphibious landing. The Admiral's ships landed the 157th Regimental Combat Team behind the American lines to support the rapid advance of the 3rd Infantry Division. The landing took place northwest of Barcellona, and was supported by the *Philadelphia, Boise, Bristol* and *Knight*; the destroyers *Wainwright, Rhind, Rowan* and *Trippe* provided a protective screen. That night American patrols entered Messina, and occupied the town the following morning. [271]

A number of amphibious landings were executed to aid American ground forces on the north coast. In addition, the Navy employed seven LCTs in a ferrying service to lift Army personnel, artillery and heavy mobile equipment from point to point along the coast. These vessels were frequently subjected to bombing and strafing by enemy aircraft. The Axis forces relied principally upon demolished bridges, blown tunnels, roadblocks and mined roads to impede the progress of advancing American forces. The Americans were able to nullify these elaborate and thorough demolitions by the exploitation of sea communications—an avenue not available to the enemy because of Allied control of the seas. In this instance, the LCTs enabled the artillery and armor to keep pace with the rapidly advancing infantry and maintain constant pressure on the retreating enemy. If these sea movements had not been made, in Hewitt's view at least, the progress of American heavy weapons would have been seriously delayed and the momentum of the American offensive considerably retarded, thereby prolonging the campaign. [272]

Admiral Hewitt's task force conducted its operations along the north coast of Sicily within 200 miles of 15 enemy airfields, four of which were within 60 miles until the fall of Catania on August 5. As a result, enemy aircraft repeatedly bombed and strafed the ships and craft operating off the north coast until the middle of August. Admiral Hewitt made an effort to limit the time the cruisers were to be in the gunfire support areas, in view of what the Admiral considered to be the inadequate air coverage provided for his naval operations. The continuity of the air coverage provided for Hewitt's task force was, in his opinion, inadequate to protect naval movements, and frequent enemy attacks were pressed home without interception by Allied fighters. The thin fighter cover provided was apparently due to an insufficient number of available aircraft to meet all air requirements. Hewitt complained that communications with fighter air coverage were inadequate. He believed this situation to be due largely to a lack of indoctrination in procedure and lack of experience on the part of both ship and air force personnel. Communications between naval commanders and the air force control stations were poor. This was aggravated by the fact that the air support command was not located at army corps headquarters, whence requests for gunfire missions originated. This resulted in loss of time in arranging for fighter cover and on some occasions, resulted in none being furnished. [273]

Catania and Troina fell during the first week of August, shrinking the front from 170 miles to about 45 miles and enabling Seventh and Eighth Armies to coordinate their attacks. Meanwhile, the enemy's flanks remained open to attack from the sea, and the Allied air forces were able to concentrate their attacks on an ever narrowing corridor of escape. Catania was softened by almost a week of heavy air bombardment, during which time over 530 bomber sorties were flown against the city. This isolated the city, and its defenses collapsed when Eighth Army, and in particular British 78th Division, seized Centuripe, thus forcing a general withdrawal. Meanwhile, between August 1 and August 6, Seventh Army was fighting an extremely bitter battle for Troina. Even though the Germans were subjected to 365 fighter-bomber sorties during the period, they still managed to organize 24 counterattacks against the American ground forces. [274]

Because of destruction caused by Allied bombing, enemy demolition, and the emplacement of countless booby traps, the advance along the north coast road was an extremely difficult one. The enemy had destroyed nearly all of the bridges between Palermo and Messina, necessitating frenzied activity by Allied combat engineers. It was, however, a series of so-called "end runs" by Allied naval forces "which largely frustrated the enemy's delaying tactics and ended by driving him from the island." Naval Task Force 88 and 3rd Infantry Division executed an amphibious landing on August 8 at San Agata to place themselves in the flank of German positions at San Fratello. The latter had halted the advance for the previous four days. Another amphibious landing was made on August 11 at Brolo, near Orlando, inhibiting German attempts to reorganize a defense system along the Naso-Cap Orlando line. Further amphibious landings were made on August 16, but these were unable to prevent the enemy's precipitous retreat. On the following day, the Allies entered Messina, thereby concluding the campaign. The campaign had cost the enemy 164,000 dead, wounded and captured (32,100

[271]  *Ibid.*
[272]  *Ibid.*, p. 77.

[273]  *Ibid.*, p. 78.
[274]  Eisenhower Dispatch, p. 30.

of whom were German), as compared with less than 20,000 Allied casualties of the same type. The enemy also lost 78 tanks and armored cars, 287 pieces of artillery and 3500 vehicles. [275]

According to Eisenhower, the Eighth Army "earned fresh renown" in the campaign, and Seventh Army had "distinguished itself by the vigor and brilliance of its fighting and its relentless pursuit action." The seminal lesson of the campaign, according to its supreme commander, was the potential for airborne operations. In spite of all of the difficulties which they had encountered, the blame for which Eisenhower shouldered himself, the Allied airborne troops had "contributed markedly to success." He concluded that "[W]e must exploit our position of superiority in air power, superiority in air transport, and availability of trained airborne troops to combine these assets with superiority in other fields, notably command of the sea and in armored forces. By so doing we can apply crushing, sudden and devastating blows that will hasten the final downfall of Nazidom." [276]

---

[275] *Ibid.*, p. 31.

[276] *Ibid.*, p. 32.

*The cruiser Boise bombards the coast of Sicily.*

*U.S. Army combat engineers and their heavy equipment disembark from an LCT at Gela, Sicily, 10 July 1943.*

*B-24 bombers blast Messina, Sicily.*

*American troops search for enemy snipers in Messina, Sicily.*

*President Roosevelt talking with Gen. H. H. Arnold, at an airfield in Sicily.*

*Generals Eisenhower and Arnold in Sicily.*

*Corporal Robert Evelyn, Redlands, California, and Pfc. Charles C. Sparlins, Vancouver, Washington (left to right), ride a foot-propelled railroad track inspection vehicle. Sicily, 13 July 1943.*

*Fires in Catania, Sicily, after an air raid by Allied bombers, June 1943.*

*Private Roy W. Humphrey of Toledo, Ohio is being given blood plasma by Pfc. Harvey White, Minneapolis, Minnesota, after he was wounded by shrapnel in Sicily on 9 August 1943. Note native woman and child in background looking on.*

*Ordnance, S.B. 4.2-inch Mortar on the Catania Plain, Sicily, August 1943.*

*Patton in Sicily.*

*Patton in Sicily.*

During the Allied invasion of Sicily the SS Robert Rowan (Liberty ship K-40) explodes after being hit by a German Ju 88 bomber off of Gela, Sicily, on 11 July 1943. Because of the cargo of ammunition the ship was abandoned without any attempt to put the fire out. Within twenty minutes the fire reached her munitions with a tremendous explosion tearing the ship in half. The burning ship came to rest on an even keel and burned for two days. The destroyer USS McLanahan (DD-615) attempted to sink the ship because the fires lit up the area during the night, but this failed as the water was too shallow.

Allied leaders in the Sicilian campaign. General Eisenhower meets in North Africa with (foreground, left to right): Air Chief Marshal Sir Arthur Tedder, General Sir Harold R. L. G. Alexander, Admiral Sir Andrew B. Cunningham, and (top row): Mr. Harold Macmillan, Major General W. Bedell Smith, and unidentified British officers.

Troops of The Loyal Edmonton Regiment entered Modica marching in a relaxed manner, but rifles are close to hand and bayonets are fixed, ready for sudden action.

*Colonel Gavin (pictured as later Maj.Gen.) led the 505th Parachute Infantry Regiment.*

*Crew from the tank "Eternity" check their vehicle after landing at Red Beach 2, Sicily, 10 July 1943.*

*Men of the 6th Durham Light Infantry chat with an American paratrooper in Avola, 11 July 1943.*

*A Renault R35 of the kind used by German forces in Sicily.*

*Men of the 2nd Seaforth Highlanders advance along a road near Noto, 11 July 1943.*

*A US Army Sherman tank moves past Sicily's rugged terrain in mid July 1943.*

*Universal carriers of the 6th Inniskillings, 38th Irish Brigade, 78th Division, in Centuripe, August 1943.*

*Infantry scramble over rubble in a devastated street in Catania, 5 August 1943.*

*American soldiers looking at a dead German pilot and his wrecked plane near Gela, Sicily, 12 July 1943.*

*Pte. Joe Makokis, Edmonton Regiment, looking at the grave of an Italian soldier. 11 July 1943, Pachino Peninsula, Italy.*

*H/Captain S.B. East, a chaplain, talking with soldiers of the 48th Highlanders of Canada near Regalbuto. 1943, Regalbuto, Sicily.*

*The initial waves of assault troops were unopposed. The military quickly established a port to bring the rest of the army onto Italian soil.*

*Specialized vessels had been developed to enable tanks to land ready for action, such as this LST disgorging an American Sherman medium tank.*

*Sgt. H.E. Cooper, 48th Highlanders of Canada. 11 August 1943, Sicily.*

*The landing in Pachino, Sicily, 10 July 1943*

*Men of the Princess Patricia's Canadian Light Infantry fighting on a ridge near Valguarnera. In the distance, enemy vehicles are burning.*

*1st Canadian Infantry Division on the road during advance on Ispica. 12 July 1943, in the vicinity of Modica, Sicily.*

*Amid heat and dust, gunners of the 7th Battery, 2nd Field Artillery Regiment, firing at enemy positions with a 25-pounder gun, Nissoria, 28 July 1943.*

*On the road to Agira, Allied jeeps driving by torched German vehicles, around 28 July 1943.*

*Infantrymen of the 48th Highlanders of Canada advancing towards Adrano. 18 August 1943, Adrano, Italy.*

*Régiment de Trois-Rivières tanks entering the ruins of Regalbuto, 4 August 1943.*

*Troops and supplies unloading near Gela on D-day.*

*81mm mortars support Patton's drive on Palermo.*

*Troina, Sicily.*

*A bunker covers the beach near Sant'Agata, Sicily.*

*Italian soldiers remove woman's body from the rubble in Palermo, May 1943.*

*Canadian forces on the move in Sicily.*

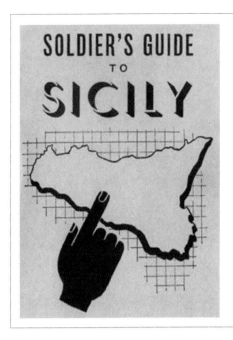

Booklet distributed to Allied troops.

U.S. and British troops landing near Gela, Sicily, 10 July 1943.

*British Lt. Gen. Bernard L. Montgomery and Lt.Gen. George S. Patton, Jr., USA, study map of Sicily, July 1943.*

*Lieutenant General George S. Patton, Jr. discusses the tactical situation with Lieutenant Colonel Lyle Bernard, 30th Infantry Regiment, commander of the second amphibious landing behind enemy lines on Sicily's north coast, near Brolo, August 1943.*

*Men of the Highland Division wade ashore from landing craft during the landings in Sicily, 10 July 1943.*

*1st Canadian Division hauling transport up from the beach, Pachino, Sicily.*

*Italian prisoners, captured while manning coastal machine gun posts, board a Royal Navy landing craft before being transported to North Africa.*

*American DUKWs standing on a pier at Licata.*

*Sicily (red) in relation to the Italian mainland.*

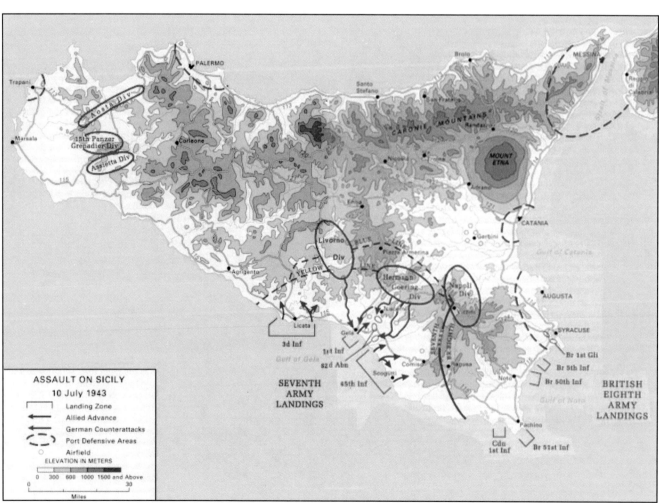

**This is a map of the Allied army amphibious landing in Sicily, 10 July 1943, as part of Operation Husky. It shows the deployments of the landing forces and the German and Italian formations defending the island.**

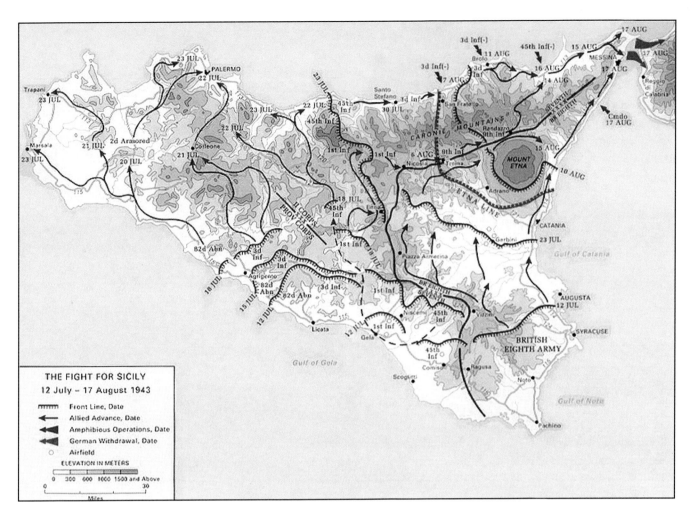

*Map of allied movements on Sicily during the month of July.*

# PERSONAL MESSAGE FROM THE ARMY COMMANDER

### To Be Read Out To All Troops.

1. The Allied Armies landed in Sicily, on Italian soil, on 10th July, magnificently supported by the Royal Navy and the Allied Air Forces, and are, today, in possession of the whole island except for the north-east corner, where the enemy is now hemmed in.

2. I want to tell all of you, soldiers of the Eighth Army, that this has been a very fine performance. On your behalf, I have expressed to the Commander of the Seventh American Army on our left the congratulations of the Eighth Army for the way the American troops have captured and cleaned up more than half the island in record time. We are proud to fight beside our American Allies.

3. The beginning has been very good, thanks to your splendid fighting qualities and to the hard work and devotion to duty of all those who work in the ports, on the roads, and in rear areas. We must not forget to give thanks to "THE LORD MIGHTY IN BATTLE" for giving us such a good beginning towards the attainment of our object.

4. And now let us get on with the job. Together with our American allies we have knocked MUSSOLINI off his perch We will now drive the Germans out of SICILY.

5. Into battle with stout hearts. Good luck to you all.

**B. L. MONTGOMERY**
General,
Eighth Army.

SICILY.
July, 1943.

*A message to the Eighth Army from General Montgomery.*

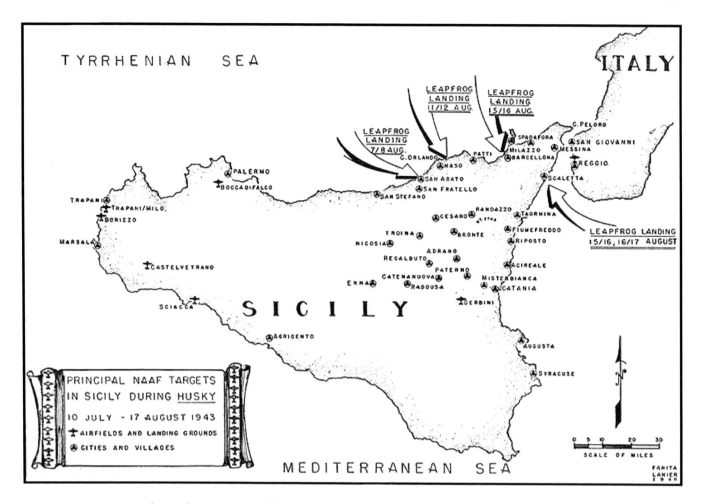

*Principle Sicilian targets of the Northwest African Air Forces for Operation Husky.*

Made in the USA
San Bernardino, CA
31 July 2013